What's in an MBA?

What's in an MBA?

THE COMPLETE GUIDE TO
MBA *and Executive MBA Programs*
IN CANADA

REBECCA **CARPENTER**

JOHN WILEY & SONS CANADA, LTD
Toronto · New York · Chichester · Weinheim · Brisbane · Singapore

Copyright © 2000 by Canadian Business Media Ltd.

All rights reserved. No part of this work covered by the copyright herein may be reproduced or used in any form or by any means—graphic, electronic or mechanical—without the prior written permission of the publisher. Any request for photocopying, recording, taping or information storage and retrieval systems of any part of this book shall be directed in writing to CANCOPY, 6 Adelaide Street East, Suite 900, Toronto, Ontario, M5A 1H6.

Care has been taken to trace ownership of copyright material contained in this book. The Publishers will gladly receive any information that will enable them to rectify any reference or credit line in subsequent editions.

John Wiley & Sons Canada Ltd
22 Worcester Road
Etobicoke, Ontario
M9W 1L1

Canadian Cataloguing in Publication Data

Carpenter, Rebecca, 1967–
   What's in an MBA? the complete guide to MBA and executive MBA programs in Canada

ISBN 0-471-64324-6

1. Business schools – Canada – Handbooks, manuals, etc. 2. Master of business administration degree – Canada – Handbooks, manuals, etc. I. Title.

HF1131.C38 1999   650'.071'171   C99-932017-3

Production Credits

Cover Design: Interrobang Graphic Design Inc.
Printer: Tri-Graphic Printing

Printed in Canada
10 9 8 7 6 5 4 3 2 1

Contents

Acknowledgements	ix
Introduction: Not All MBAs Are Created Equal	xi

Part I: What's An MBA Worth to You? — 1

Chapter 1: The MBA: Frequently Asked Questions	3
Chapter 2: How to Determine the Financial Benefits of Your MBA	11
Chapter 3: Distance MBAs	25
Chapter 4: Co-op MBAs	33

Part II: Business School Profiles — 41

University of Alberta	43
MBA	44
Executive MBA	48
Athabasca University	51
MBA	52
MBA in Agriculture	54

University of British Columbia	57
MBA	59
MBA in Financial Services	62
University of Calgary	67
MBA	68
Executive MBA	72
Concordia University	77
MBA	79
Aviation MBA	82
Executive MBA	83
Dalhousie University	87
MBA	89
MBA in Financial Services	92
MBA in Information Technology	92
University of Guelph	97
MBA in Agriculture	98
Electronic MBA in Agriculture	99
École des Hautes Études Commerciales	103
MBA	105
Laurentian University	111
MBA	112
Université Laval	117
MBA	119
University of Manitoba	125
MBA	126
McGill University	133
MBA	135
McMaster University	143
MBA	144
Memorial University	153
MBA	154
Université de Moncton	161
MBA	162
University of New Brunswick—Fredricton	167
MBA	168
University of New Brunswick—Saint John	173
MBA	174

University of Ottawa	177
MBA	178
International MBA	180
Executive MBA	181
Université du Québec à Montréal	185
MBA	186
MBA in Financial Services	188
MBA in Real Estate Management	189
Executive MBA	189
Queen's University	193
MBA	194
National Executive MBA	199
Executive MBA in Ottawa	199
University of Regina	203
MBA	204
Royal Roads University	209
MBA	210
Saint Mary's University	213
MBA	214
Executive MBA	216
University of Saskatchewan	221
MBA	222
Unversité de Sherbrooke	229
MBA	230
Executive MBA	233
Simon Fraser University	237
MBA	238
MBA in Financial Services	242
Management of Technology MBA	243
Executive MBA	243
University of Toronto	247
MBA	249
Executive MBA	253
University of Victoria	257
MBA	258
University of Western Ontario	265
MBA	267

Executive MBA	271
Wilfrid Laurier University	277
MBA	278
Sarnia MBA	282
Laurier on the Lakeshore MBA	282
University of Windsor	285
MBA	286
York University	293
MBA	295

Acknowledgements

I am greatly indebted to numerous students and alumni who were generous with their time and their opinions. This guide could not have been completed without the cooperation of deans and program directors, who often found themselves scrounging for information no one had ever asked for previously. I am grateful to the staff of *Canadian Business*: in particular, Arthur Johnson, who proposed this project to me; Cristina Brandao and Nancy Carr, who checked numbers and made reminder calls; David Berman, who allowed me to include his article on co-op MBAs in this volume; and, especially, Ian McGugan, who commented on the manuscript and made many improvements. Karen Milner and Elizabeth McCurdy, my editors at John Wiley & Sons, have been extremely helpful in making this book more reader-friendly. I would like to thank Michael Kennedy for many useful conversations on business school taxonomy. I am obliged to Pramila David for tape transcription and data-entry. I cannot imagine completing this project without Richard Laxton, who lived through this book alongside me, put my computer back together several times, and was unwavering in his support. Finally, I would like to thank my parents, Adrienne and Stirling Carpenter, for their love and encouragement.

Introduction
Not All MBAs Are Created Equal

Five years ago, if you'd asked anyone to define what an MBA means, chances are they would have told you that MBA programs are two years long and teach general management. They might have added that doing an MBA prepares you for a comfortable slot in a big corporation. "You got on the train with your ticket, which was the MBA, and 40 years later you got off and were given your gold watch," says Herman Smith of Herman Smith Executive Initiative Inc., an executive search firm based in Toronto.

But in the past five years, MBA programs have undergone more changes than they have in the past five decades. These changes have affected every aspect of the degree. Programs now run anywhere from 11 months to two years and four months. The focus, in many cases, is on specific industries or skills rather than on general management. Methods of delivery have been overhauled completely, with several schools teaching courses over the Internet or via videoconferencing. Joint degrees, once available solely in law and business, have proliferated: an MBA can now be blended with a Master of Fine Arts or with an MD, to name but two combinations.

The upheaval means that one MBA may now bear only a slight resemblance to another MBA. How do you compare a co-op program like the one at McMaster University with the University of Western Ontario's general management program or with Athabasca University's electronic format? You can't and you're not meant to, because the three cater to completely different markets. McMaster targets young students with minimal work experience, Western wants those with three or four years of work experience, while Athabasca students have, on average, nine years of managerial experience. "The MBA has lost stature," says David Conrath, dean of the Michael G. DeGroote School of Business at McMaster. "By itself it used to mean something. Now you have to market a specific MBA."

Schools have done so with gusto. In a cutthroat market in which everyone competes, small, specialized programs have become the favourite way for business schools to differentiate themselves from the pack. A side benefit for the schools is that new programs can often be priced at cost and used to finance existing programs—a consideration in provinces such as Quebec and British Columbia where tuition fees for old programs start low and can only be increased by a small margin each year.

The Trend Toward Specialization

The trend toward specialization has some benefits for students. Specialized MBAs give people an opportunity to develop the precise mix of skills that employers in a particular industry need. Executive recruiter Herman Smith says programs such as the MBA in financial services at Dalhousie University are really "trade MBAs" and predicts that they "will give students a leg up in that particular market." Queen's

MBA for Science & Technology has allowed many people stuck in modestly paid scientific jobs to double their pre-MBA salary while remaining in their field of choice.

Not everything is without flaws, however. As schools have stretched the definition of an MBA, they have also stretched the requirements necessary to complete the degree. At one end of the spectrum are Queen's and the University of Toronto, where students entering MBA programs in 1998 recorded the highest average GMATs in the schools' histories (648 and 660, respectively). At the other extreme is Athabasca's MBA program. It recorded an average GMAT of 566 among entering students in 1995, but saw this figure drop to 535 in 1996. Last year the school decided that the GMAT was no longer relevant (because its students have lots of work experience), and stopped requiring the test. Meanwhile, some schools are pushing the specialization of their programs into uncharted territory. Royal Roads University in Victoria, one of the newest universities in Canada, is launching four new executive MBA programs, including an MBA in public relations and communications.

Buyer Beware

The question arises: when does an MBA stop being an MBA? When it's six months long? And when does a specialized MBA become so narrow that it's no longer a management degree but vocational training? As competition for students heats up, the temptation increases for schools to reduce admission requirements. So does the temptation for schools to create programs that are so narrowly focused that they betray the general "management" tag in the degree's name.

Students and employers should be aware that all MBAs are no longer created equal. For students, the increased diversity among MBAs means that you need to choose the program that best corresponds to your interests and projected career path. You must look at the school, its admission standards, and its placement record, because "the name of the place and the quality of the place is something you're going to have to live with for a very long time," says Derek Atkins, a professor in the School of Commerce and Business Administration at the University of British Columbia.

While most employers are still impressed by the MBA, many have yet to come to grips with the proliferation of specialized variants. "An MBA carries a lot of weight, but it doesn't seal the deal," says Craig Hemer, a partner with Ray & Berndtson, an executive search firm based in Vancouver. So far, his clients have asked only for the generic MBA; he's never had anyone say, "now if we had someone with an MBA with a specialty in marketing or information technology, that would really clinch things."

Some headhunters believe there's room for a range of MBAs, from general management degrees to narrowly specialized programs. "There are some organizations going the lean-and-mean way that want to have people who can work in a number of different areas. Larger organizations, by virtue of their size, want someone who can specialize. It really varies with the industry and the organization and, very often, the philosophy of the CEO," says Lyn Landreville, research manager at Davies Park Executive Search Consultants in Calgary.

But caveat emptor. If business schools continue to drop their admission requirements, and focus their programs on narrow specialities, employers are likely to start taking a closer look at credentials and demanding to know which school a candidate attended and what he or she studied. Business schools should play an active role in keeping standards high. Otherwise, can a five-month MBA in paper-clip management be far behind?

Choosing the Program that's Right for You

What's in an MBA? will help you choose the MBA or the EMBA that's right for you. Part I of this book, which brings together articles from the last two issues of *Canadian Business'* highly touted MBA package, will answer some preliminary questions you should ask yourself before you embark on an MBA. What sort of financial payback can you expect from an MBA? should you choose a one-year or a two-year program? who should enroll in a distance program? and so forth. Part II features in-depth profiles of 32 MBA programs with information on programs and specializations, admissions and payoff, social life and extracurriculars, as well as fun facts about each program, such as famous alumni and companies started by grads.

All figures, except where noted, pertain to the 1997-98 academic year. Programs and figures change constantly, so be aware that in most cases, tuition fees and starting salaries will be higher than what we have stated. Use our contact information and website information to get more details on the programs you're interested in.

PART I

What's An MBA to You?

CHAPTER ONE

The MBA
Frequently Asked Questions

Do I need an MBA to get a good job?

Here's some good news: an MBA is not an absolute requirement, even in typical MBA jobs such as management consulting. McKinsey & Co. of Toronto, the blue-chip consulting firm, drew on MBAs for less than 50% of its 1996 recruits, while 1997 recruits included a slightly larger proportion of business grads.

Here's the bad news: you still need top-drawer qualifications to get hired. In addition to business graduates, McKinsey likes to employ Rhodes scholars, lawyers, and doctors of engineering, medicine or other sciences. Other consulting firms are just as picky.

Luckily, in many business sectors, the bar is quite a bit lower. Only 10% of Procter & Gamble's recruits last year had an MBA. Similarly, Kraft Canada hired 14 people last year for entry-level positions in finance and marketing, and only three of them had an MBA. These packaged-goods firms like to hire young graduates and then shape them in their own molds.

Consequently, an undergraduate degree in business can be as good a ticket to a job with these companies as an MBA.

> The MBA seems to be most prized in finance firms. Says Paul Rogers, head of investment banking at CIBC Wood Gundy: "The MBA is an extraordinarily useful tool. We think there is a perfect mapping [between what MBA students are taught and our firm's mission to create value]."

The paradox is that while an MBA isn't an absolute requirement, plenty of MBA graduates say they would not have their current job without the degree. Undertaken at the proper time, an MBA can be the quickest—although not the only—door opener to a number of careers. Take Philip King, a University of Toronto MBA, who graduated into a job with a hefty income at the management consulting firm of A. T. Kearney. Without the degree, he says, "I would have needed the motivation and sophistication to approach the firm on my own." With the MBA, King had "some pedigree." Even more than the contacts or the specific knowledge, the MBA is particularly useful in combination with something else. Especially prized are engineers and scientists who can add an MBA perspective to their technical expertise.

When is the best time to do an MBA?

If your motivations are primarily financial, the best time to do an MBA is after three to five years of work experience. At that point, you are somewhat seasoned, and an MBA can deliver big benefits for several reasons:

- You probably won't be leaving behind a big salary to go back to school.

- You will have a long career during which you can enjoy the benefits of an MBA and amortize the cost of going back to school.

- You're at the right age when you graduate to be attractive to the highest-paying employers—investment banks and consulting firms.

If, on the other hand, you're coming straight from undergrad and have no work experience to speak of you might want to consider a co-op MBA program. For people with 10 years' experience and family obligations, it's a different story again. They should look into distance MBAs or EMBAs, which will allow them to study part-time.

Should I do a one-year or a two-year MBA?

One-year MBA programs are becoming increasingly attractive, especially for those who have already been working for a few years. Shorter programs are easier on the pocketbook since you pass up only one year of salary instead of two. They also give you just as many employment opportunities as two-year programs. Many top consulting firms and investment banks have long recruited at one-year European programs such as the internationally acclaimed INSEAD in France, and draw no distinction between one-year and two-year program grads. "I'm not sure that there's a big difference between a one-year and a two-year program," says Brent Snell, principal at A.T. Kearney. "One-year programs are going to attract students who are very focused. But if you don't have much work experience, a two-year degree may be better, because students will be maturing during those two years."

Maja Dettbarn, director of North American resourcing for several CIBC-related companies, including CIBC Wood Gundy Securities Inc. in Toronto, admits to a slight bias toward two-year programs, although the firm hires from both kinds of programs: "I believe one of the ways you learn is by grasping and touching things, and you can't really do that in one year."

Other MBA employers, such as Procter & Gamble and Kraft Canada, have no preference for a two-year MBA over a one-year program. As for the high-tech industry, it's so desperate for applicants with both business and technical skills that the sooner it gets them, the better. "As a general rule, I prefer a one-year program that is focused on the needs of the industry because we get the students after only one year," says Claudine Simson, assistant vice-president for global external research and intellectual property at Northern Telecom Ltd. of Mississauga, Ontario.

> The following schools offer programs that are one year in length:
> - École des Hautes Études Commerciales
> - University of Manitoba
> - University of New Brunswick at Saint John
> - Queen's University
> - Wilfrid Laurier University
>
> In addition, several schools such as the University of British Columbia and the University of Ottawa have reduced the length of their MBA by less than a year, enabling their students to graduate in 15 months. Other schools grant advanced placement to candidates with substantial academic background in business, allowing them to cut the length of time they spend in the program.

Should I do a part-time or a full-time MBA?

If your circumstances are such that you can't take time off to attend school full time, you might want to consider doing a part-time MBA. Research has shown that part-time grads also experience pay increases, although not as high as those received by full-timers. (The main reason for this is that current employers are sometimes reluctant to recognize new skills an employee has acquired through an MBA program.) Studying part-time means that you have no opportunity costs and that course material is immediately applicable. Furthermore, many employers will sponsor employees for a part-time MBA.

One drawback of a part-time MBA is that you tend to be out of the loop as far as the recruiting circuit is concerned. Career-placement offices, on the whole, do not lavish much attention on part-timers. A second caveat is that some of the highest-paying jobs, particularly with consulting firms, are much harder to get if you aren't a full-time student. As a part-timer, you are seen as being overripe for induction into the consulting culture, where they like you mature but still malleable. "The younger we bring them in, the more readily we can bring them into our culture," says Paul ter Weeme, a partner in Mitchell Madison Group, a management consulting firm based in New York.

Part-time and Full-time Programs

UNIVERSTIY	PART-TIME	FULL-TIME
Alberta	x	x
Athabasca	x	–
UBC	x	x
Calgary	x	x
Concordia	x	x
Dalhousie	x	x
Guelph	x	x
HEC	x	x
Laurentian	x	x
Laval	x	x
Manitoba	x	x
McGill	x	x
McMaster	x	x
Memorial	x	x
Moncton	x	x
New Brunswick-Fredricton	x	x
New Brunswick-Saint John	x	x
Ottawa	x	x

Quebec à Montreal	–	x
Queen's	–	x
Regina	x	x
Royal Roads	x	–
Saint Mary's	x	x
Saskatchewan	x	x
Simon Fraser	–	x
Sherbrook	x	x
Toronto	x	x
Victoria	x	x
Western	–	x
Wilfrid Laurier	x	x
Windsor	x	x
York	x	x

What About Executive MBAs?

If you already have several years of work experience, an Executive MBA (EMBA) program, which typically allows you to earn an MBA in two years of intensive weekend and part-time study, may provide the best value of all—particularly if the firm you're already employed by is willing to spring for the cost of tuition. Danny Shapiro, director of the EMBA program at Simon Fraser University in Burnaby, BC—the longest-running program of its kind in Canada—hasn't formally surveyed his grads on their financial payoff. He says, though, that it's not uncommon for participants to receive a promotion upon admission to the program.

Other insiders say it's a bit of a dirty secret among EMBA directors that some grads move on to other jobs after the degree. As a result, some sponsoring employers have started asking employees to sign a document promising to stay for a certain number of years after graduation. But in any case, the outlook for EMBAs is good. Your current employer is likely to treat you well because a lot has been invested in you; a new employer may think you're special because your previous employer thought you were special enough to be sent to an EMBA course. "When I bump into grads five years down the road, they're pretty happy people," says Shapiro.

EMBA Programs
The following universities offer EMBA programs.

- Alberta
- Calgary
- Concordia
- Ottawa
- Quebec à Montreal
- Queen's
- Saint Mary's
- Simon Fraser
- Sherbrooke
- Toronto
- Western

CHAPTER TWO

How to Determine the Financial Benefits of Your MBA

When Philip King enrolled in the University of Toronto's MBA program in the fall of 1995, he hardly knew what management consulting was. The Tennessee native had graduated from Harvard University in 1992 with a major in US history. Then he worked in New York with the Edison Project, an organization involved in the privatization of public schools. That experience whetted his interest in commerce and when his wife, Leta, a Canadian schoolteacher, returned to her job in Toronto, he decided to investigate U of T's business program. What clinched his decision to enroll was the unbelievably low cost of Canadian tuition by US standards. "I thought, 'I can't pass this up,'" says King.

King's experience provides dramatic evidence of the financial payoff from attaining an MBA. Barely 30, he works as an associate consultant for A.T. Kearney Ltd. in Toronto. He makes a salary almost double his pre-MBA pay and is on track to earn a $100,000-plus compensation package within a couple of years. Yet he insists he hadn't really counted on making piles of money, and is amazed at his good fortune: "I feel like I tripped over this opportunity. I feel very lucky and almost undeserving."

As King's story demonstrates, people go to business school for a wide variety of reasons. Many discover they have a latent interest in business. Others regard the MBA degree as an intellectual challenge or as a way to increase their career flexibility. But unlike students in many other disciplines, they also have some immediate payback in mind. Most are motivated, at least in part, by the desire for a better job and a hefty paycheque. For them, there is always a fundamental accounting question to consider: does an MBA make financial sense?

Strangely enough, that question doesn't get addressed in B-school promotional pamphlets. But no self-respecting business school would recommend that you go into a new business venture without making a five-year plan. Likewise, no business school book would tell you to enter an MBA program without doing a thorough cost/benefit analysis.

In the last two MBA issues of *Canadian Business*, we've tried to determine which MBAs make you money or cost you money in the years after graduation. As general as our numbers are, they hint at some surprising conclusions. For those already earning good salaries, there can be amazingly little payoff from completing some MBA programs. It may be years before your MBA pays you back for the total cost of attending school, especially if you're earning $45,000 or more.

Another surprise is how much business schools vary in their financial benefits. While some programs offer dubious paybacks, especially to those already earning good incomes, the top graduates from a handful of programs can count on recouping the cost of their MBAs, including tuition and lost salary, within a couple of years of leaving the classroom. Sometimes the payback from these top schools can be spectacular. In 1997 a student from the Richard Ivey School of Business at the University of Western Ontario attracted a starting salary (including bonus) of $230,000—by all accounts, a record for a Canadian MBA graduate. At Western, U of T, and Queen's, six-figure starting salaries aren't uncommon.

Money Machines

One way to judge a school is by how much it raises students' salary. Only five schools track that information—but the numbers are impressive.

UNIVERSITY	Average entering salaries	Average starting salaries
Ottawa	$50,287	$55,568
Queen's	$42,700	$75,059
Western	$46,000	$74,000
Wilfrid Laurier	$44,000	$58,000
York	$42,000	$76,000

Of course, money isn't everything. The advantages of attending a business school in your hometown or one that offers a particular strength in your chosen area of specialization may outweigh the general figures outlined here. But be aware of the financial implications of your decision. Canadian business schools are in a state of upheaval. Several are experimenting with different program lengths, higher tuition fees, and more specialized curricula. As MBA programs become more diverse, it makes more sense than ever to pause a second and ask yourself a very simple question: what is the MBA of your choice really worth?

Nineteen Degrees of Separation

Canadian MBA programs have become more varied in recent years, with some schools drastically cutting the length of their courses or raising tuition.

UNIVERSITY	time in program	total tuition and fees	average starting salary	median starting salary	salary range	size of sample
Alberta	20 months	$8,600	$63,913	$58,000	$30K-$120K	52 out of 60
UBC	15 months	$7,000	$60,200	$55,000	$40K-$104K	62 out of 86
Calgary*	20 months	$9,080	$61,043	N/A	$30K-$135K	61 out of 92
Concordia	20 months	$6,842	$50,000	$48,000	$38K-$120K	33 out of 74

UNIVERSITY	time in program	total tuition and fees	average starting salary	median starting salary	salary range	size of sample
Dalhousie*	20 months	$9,950	$52,500	$50,150	$35K-$80K	30 out of 85
HEC	12 months	$6,000	$60,000	N/A	$35K-$120K	85 out of 90
McGill	20 months	$7,336	$70,000	$65,000	$48K-$150K	102 out of 140
McMaster*•	28 months	$11,328	$56,615	N/A	$38K-$95K	44 out of 51
Manitoba	11 months	$17,600	$72,500	N/A	N/A	43 out of 48
Moncton	20 months	$6,600	$36,000	$45,000	$28K-$60K	25 out of 60
Ottawa*	15 months	$8,892	$55,568	$55,455	$20K-$156K	66 out of 195
Queen's	12 months	$26,500	$75,059	$70,000	$46K-$145K	44 out of 55
Saint Mary's*	20 months	$9,168	$43,500	$43,000	$33K-US$110K	71 out of 71
Sherbrooke§	16 months	$3,615	$44,143	$44,000	$31K-$55K	N/A
Toronto	20 months	$16,116	$78,000	N/A	$45K-$176K	85 out of 107
Western	20 months	$26,000	$74,000	N/A	$45K-$140K	144 out of 197
W.Laurier†	12 months	$7,420	$58,800	$53,000	$42K-$90K	36 out of 78
Windsor*•	24 months	$9,400	$45,000	$48,500	$35K-$75K	43 out of 50
York	20 months	$8,552	$76,000	$73,000	$42K-$257K	181 out of 472

* 1997 figures; § 1996 figures; † combination of 1995 and 1996 numbers; • co-op grads

The MBA Advantage

Ronald Yeaple, a professor at the University of Rochester's business school in New York state, may have been the first person to take a cold-blooded look at the value of a business education. In 1994, he wrote a book called *The MBA Advantage: Why It Pays to Get an MBA*, in which he ranked 20 top US business schools according to the financial return they gave their graduates. The so-called "MBA advantage" of each school was the cumulative amount that a typical member of the class of '92 could expect to earn in the five years following graduation, after subtracting tuition fees and what the student would have made without the MBA.

Yeaple's ranking presents a very different view of business schools from *Business Week's* widely quoted ratings, which are based upon surveys of graduates and corporate recruiters.

Northwestern University in Illinois, for instance, placed only sixth in Yeaple's book, despite its first-place showing in the *Business Week* rankings. Yale University, which hadn't even made the *Business Week* list, rose to fifth. Yeaple's calculations cast some harsh light on just how big—or small—the payback from an MBA can be. Five years after graduating from B-school, a typical Harvard grad (Yeaple's No. 1 school) had an MBA advantage of US$133,647, while a typical graduate from New York University—Yeaple's lowest-ranked school—had an advantage of only US$4,121. Adjust for taxes and discount the annual return to account for the time value of money, and the differences were even more dramatic: the Harvard grad was ahead by US$148,378 five years after graduation, while the NYU grad actually lost US$3,749 by attending business school.

Applying Yeaple's method to Canadian MBA schools yields cruder results, mainly because of the lack of data. Only five Canadian schools—Queen's, the University of Ottawa, Western, York, and Wilfrid Laurier University—provide figures for student salaries before enrollment. Amazingly, several Canadian B-schools still keep no data on what students earn after graduation—which means they have to be excluded altogether from this analysis.

Making matters more difficult is the diverse nature of Canadian MBA students. In the US, the top business schools tend to draw from a very homogeneous pool of applicants in their mid-20s with four or five years of work experience. In Canada, the difference between students at various schools is far greater. Students at Wilfrid Laurier's MBA program, for instance, tend to be five years older on average than students at Western. The age difference means the average Western grad will have a longer career over which to enjoy the benefits of the MBA than the typical Wilfrid Laurier grad.

For all of these reasons, our payback calculations can't be regarded as a ranking of the relative merit or academic quality of the business schools. Instead, it's better to regard these numbers as a general indicator of the return you can expect on your education dollar during the first five years after graduation.

The Methodology

Here's the way our methodology works. Because programs now vary so widely in length, we looked at students' payback during the seven years from the time they enter their chosen program. In other words, if you plan to start school in the fall of 2000, our analysis should give you a good idea of what your financial payback will be in the fall of 2007, regardless of whether you've chosen a one-year program or a 20-month program. We've also taken into account what an MBA student in a 20-month program can earn during the summer months and what a co-op student can earn during work terms. Those amounts can be quite significant. In McMaster University's co-op MBA, for example, work-term salaries allow a student to earn as much as $56,000 over the course of the program.

We've tried to make our analysis as comprehensive as possible by taking into account the widely varying salaries that MBA students give up to do their degrees. This is a vital factor to consider because the higher the salary you are earning now, the more it costs you, in terms of forgone paycheques, to get your MBA. To account for this disparity, we evaluated each school's financial payback for three hypothetical students: one who would have left behind a salary of $25,000 to do an MBA, another who would have given up a $35,000 salary; and a third who would have surrendered a $45,000 income to go to b-school.

We began by calculating the total income each of these students would have earned seven years after enrolling in an MBA program. In the case of one-year MBA programs, we estimated cumulative earnings for six post-MBA years. In the case of traditional 20-month programs, we estimated total earnings for the five years and four months after graduation. We added to this figure a total for summer or co-op earnings, assuming that our students could earn $12,000 in either a summer of work or in a four-month work term. Finally, we estimated what students would have earned in the same seven-year period without an MBA, and added the cost of tuition to that figure. We subtracted the second figure from the first to find out how far ahead—or behind—an MBA puts you.

Since no school surveys grads' salaries five years down the line, we proceeded on the assumption that each of our hypothetical students would land a job at the average salary for a school's graduates, then increase their pay packet by 10% a year after graduation. In contrast, we assumed that their pay would increase at an annual rate of only 5% if they did not do an MBA. While those assumptions are arbitrary, we believe they tilt our calculations heavily in favor of MBA programs: in essence, we are saying that MBAs will move up the salary food-chain twice as fast as non-MBAs.

To make our task manageable, we had to assume that our hypothetical students were average. They did not fast-forward through a program thanks to advanced standing. If they were in a 20-month program, they were employed during the four-month summer term. Unfortunately, a few schools had to be excluded from our analysis because they still don't track their grads' performance in the job market.

Our Findings

1. **Queen's MBA for Science & Technology delivers the best return.** Tuition is steep because the program is fully privatized, but the $26,500 bill is more than made up for by the third-highest starting salaries in Canada and the fact that students in the 12-month program need to forgo earning an income for only one year. Though the program prepares people for work in the high-tech sector, employers still come from a broad spectrum of companies. In fact, management consulting firms were the largest single employers of the class of '98, a factor which no doubt helped propel salaries upward.

2. **The University of Manitoba's 11-month MBA takes second place.** We should point out that students in Manitoba's MBA program tend to be a special breed: the average age of full-time students is 35, and most have about 11 years of work experience, which may help to explain their high starting salaries.

Who's in first?

Queen's, that's who. But our analysis shows that several other schools are close behind. We've calculated below how much richer—or poorer—an MBA leaves students seven years after entering school. To make our numbers as precise as possible, we've looked at the payback for students earning $25,000, $35,000, and $45,000 before entering school. One surprise: the rating of each school remained the same, regardless of the student's entering paycheque.

UNIVERSITY	salary of $25,000	Rating	salary of $35,000	Rating	salary of $45,000	Rating
Alberta	224,351	10	142,930	10	61,869	10
UBC	229,691	9	148,270	9	67,209	9
Calgary	204,831	11	123,391	11	42,330	11
Concordia	133,704	16	52,283	16	-28,778	16
Dalhousie	147,202	13	165,781	13	-13,280	13
HEC	253,386	7	171,965	7	90,904	7
McGill	253,386	6	184,628	6	103,567	6
McMaster	139,134	15	57,713	15	-23,350	15
Manitoba	338,230	2	256,809	2	175,748	2
Moncton	52,959	19	-28,462	19	-109,523	19
Ottawa	193,925	12	112,504	12	31,443	12
Queen's	349,072	1	267,651	1	186,590	1
Saint Mary's	88,377	17	6,956	17	-74,105	17
Sherbrooke	139,649	14	58,228	14	-22,833	14
Toronto	310,404	3	228,983	3	147,922	3
Western	273,952	5	192,531	5	111,470	5
W.Laurier†	244,781	8	163,360	8	82,299	8
Windsor	85,779	18	4,358	18	-76,703	18
York	304,685	4	223,264	4	142,203	4

3. **University of Toronto grads had the highest average starting salaries in Canada, a factor that helped carry the school to a third-place finish in our study.** U of T's tuition is also quite reasonable—for now. In 1998 it increased its tuition to $8,058 for year one of its two-year program from $5,500, a figure that puts it in the mid-range for Canadian

MBA programs. But new dean Roger Martin has signaled that fees will increase. U of T used to be a finance enclave, sending half its graduating class into that sector. In 1998, for the first time, consulting firms claimed 26% of grads, the same percentage as investment banks. The school has long attracted Wall Street investment banks, and those banks have now begun to hire directly for their New York offices rather than for their Canadian outposts. The program turned out several grads with starting salaries of more than $100,000.

4. **In fourth place, an MBA from York's Schulich School of Business is a bargain.** The school charges only $8,552 in tuition for the complete program, compared to U of T's $16,116, Queen's $26,500, Manitoba's $17,600, and the University of Western Ontario's $26,000. Yet the average starting salaries of York grads are the second highest of any Canadian MBA program. Dezsö Horváth, dean of the school, maintains that he has no immediate plans to privatize the school and that Schulich's tuition rates will remain low to keep the program accessible. The school has a flexible setup that allows students to move at will between part-time and full-time options. Classes run on the trimester system so full-time students can complete an MBA in 16 months of non-stop study if they choose.

5. **The Richard Ivey School of Business at the University of Western Ontario is still a lot of people's choice as Canada's most prestigious MBA program.** It finished only fifth in our payback analysis—tuition is high at $26,000 and the program is two years in length—but chances are you won't be disappointed by the program's results, regardless of your entering salary. The school's starting salary is a respectable $74,000, the fourth highest in Canada, and Ivey is striving to raise it even higher. The school recently revamped its placement office and now has eight full-timers, including three so-called relationship managers: one with expertise in consulting, the second in investment banking, and the third in the packaged goods industry.

We conclude with a reminder that these figures should not be treated as a carved-in-stone ranking of business schools. First, some schools provided salary figures for 1997, while others already had 1998 figures. Since 1998 salaries tend to be higher, our results probably understate the payback potential of certain schools. Second, our assumptions can't take into account the different student populations at various MBA programs. Students at Windsor, for instance, generally have no work experience at all—the student with an entering salary of $45,000 would be an anomaly—while those at Wilfrid Laurier come in with an average of eight years of experience. Finally, remember that there is a wide range in each school's starting salary. It's entirely possible for someone to go to a school not among our top five and emerge with an impressive starting salary: $156,000 at the University of Ottawa or $120,000 at École des Hautes Études Commerciales (HEC). But you can also graduate from a top-ranked school into a middling salary of $45,000. To find out how much richer or poorer an MBA can make you, plug your circumstances into our equation and examine the results.

Six Steps to Six Figures

Our MBA payback figures show that high starting salaries translate into big payoffs. No surprise there. But what do high starting salaries depend on? Herewith, some guidelines to securing the biggest bucks possible.

1. *Don't be 23 years old.*

Get some work experience before enrolling in an MBA. The lowest starting salaries are found in programs such as those offered by the University of Windsor or McMaster University, which accept hordes of students straight from undergraduate programs. These MBAs are designed to give students work experience through co-ops, but a couple of work terms are usually insufficient to endear inexperienced grads to the highest-paying employers.

2. Choose a place with a good name.

Some of the highest starting salaries are found at Western, Queen's, and Toronto. Prestigious programs are more likely to have alumni in senior positions. They may also benefit from the borrowed glory that comes from being part of a well-known university. Yeaple mentions a study that asked senior executives to rate the reputations of various US business schools. Predictably, Harvard and Stanford scored high, but so did Princeton University—which has no business school.

3. Look for a program with a Type-A placement office.

An aggressive placement office can play a big role in persuading companies to recruit on-campus, says Michael Kennedy, a consultant and former MBA placement officer with McGill University. You should choose a business school that operates its own placement office and can target recruiters directly, rather than picking a program that relies on a centralized placement office that caters to every program in the university. To find out which schools shine at the recruiting game, get the career placement records. Check the figures for starting salaries. Look at which companies hired last year; chances are they'll show up this year as well. "We try to measure the return we get from recruiting at a particular campus. If we haven't been able to hire a top grad in two years, we might downgrade the school," says Brent Snell, who recruits for A.T. Kearney Ltd. in Toronto.

4. Follow the consulting firms and investment banks.

Scan the highest starting salary for each school and if it's a six-digit figure, you're looking at a fresh recruit for a consulting firm or an investment bank. Lots of schools can't draw these choosy people. Consulting firm Mitchell

Madison Group of New York, for instance, will recruit for the first time at Canadian schools this fall and plans to visit Western, McGill, and Queen's. "We're not going to 15 schools because it's an enormous expense," says Paul ter Weeme, a partner in the firm. "We're going where we think we're going to find who we want."

5. *Make the dean's list.*

"There is a subset of people in the class that every consulting firm and every investment bank wants to hire," says ter Weeme. To be one of those people, you need top grades, combined with equal parts charm, drive, and quant skills. Mediocre results screen you out immediately from the highest-paying jobs.

6. *Stay away from Montreal, B.C., and the Maritimes.*

Salaries tend to be lower in these areas. In addition, Montreal is crawling with MBAs from the nearby universities of Sherbrooke, Laval, and Ottawa, not to mention the four MBA programs right in the city: McGill, Concordia University, Université du Québec à Montréal, and École des Hautes Études Commerciales. "There's a huge unemployment problem in Montreal. The MBA is not a major advantage," says Kennedy. Salaries are higher in Toronto and in the US, particularly in New York. In addition, US firms are more likely to provide signing bonuses, says Jane Flynn, former director of the career management centre at U of T's business school.

Does all of this mean that you should pass up doing an MBA if there is no clear-cut financial gain? No, but what it does indicate is that you should be clear about your motivation. If your primary goal is to expand your horizons or open up new career prospects, the degree can still be valuable—even if the financial payback may be questionable.

Consider the case of Alf Sailer. In 1994, at the age of 39, he sold his profitable dental practice to enroll in the MBA program at the University of Calgary. As a dentist, he had been working about 29 hours a week and taking home more than $100,000 a year. But he was bored by the routine and knew he didn't want to continue looking at teeth for the rest of his working life.

Sailer was interested in learning more about investing wisely, but he was also intrigued by the oil and gas industry. After a year in the MBA program, he realized, "I'm never going to learn oil and gas. I'm almost 40. There are guys my age who've been in the industry for 20 years." Instead, he parlayed his science background into a job as a life sciences specialist for Acumen Capital Finance Partners Ltd. of Calgary, an investment dealer that, among other things, helps fledgling biotech companies find financing.

A year after graduation, Sailer is already approaching what he made as a dentist. And he says he is entirely satisfied by the opportunities his MBA has opened up, despite the fact that he is now working three times as many hours as he did as a dentist. Does he ever regret his decision? "No way. What I'm doing now is too much fun," he says. "In all fairness, it's still all new and exciting. Dentistry for the first seven years was fun also. But there's far more variety in what I'm doing now."

CHAPTER THREE

Distance MBAs

Sharon Ritchie, a senior manager at Royal Bank of Canada, brings along her laptop computer whenever she drives her son to his hockey games. While her son warms up with his team, Ritchie sits in the car chatting electronically to her classmates in Athabasca University's on-line MBA program. Then she goes in to watch the game. Two hours later, while her son is changing back into his street clothes, she returns to the car and works on a group assignment until he emerges for the drive home.

Nobody forced Ritchie to do her MBA this way. A high-school graduate who started working at Royal Bank as a teller 21 years ago, she lives in Toronto and could have attended a traditional classroom, complete with flesh-and-blood professors and classmates. Since her employer was footing the bill, money was no object for her. In fact, Ritchie had already been accepted into University of Toronto's prestigious executive MBA program when a co-worker told her about the Athabasca option.

The Flexible Alternative

Ritchie was intrigued. What clinched her decision to attend Athabasca's innovative program was finding out that it would require only 20 to 30 hours of work a week over three years. By comparison, U of T's course was far more intense— 40 to 60 hours a week for two years. What's more, by choosing the Athabasca alternative, Ritchie would be able to do all her course work from home, over the Internet. "I had a commitment from my husband and family, but I was worried about the hours involved in going to U of T," she says. "Taking the degree at Athabasca meant I'd have peace and sanity."

Like Ritchie, many MBA students across Canada are taking a close look at what the new field of distance education has to offer. Some students are choosing to do their MBA via the Internet or videoconferencing simply because there is no traditional MBA program near where they live. Others, though, are opting for distance education because it offers unparalleled flexibility. While distance MBAs are only five years old in Canada, there are already several programs to choose from, each with its own distinct classroom culture and teaching technology.

The Long-Distance Feeling

Queen's University pioneered the field when it began offering an MBA via videoconferencing in 1994; the school now operates sites in 24 cities. The Richard Ivey School of Business at the University of Western Ontario followed Queen's move in 1995 and now operates seven videoconferencing sites. Athabasca University, based in Athabasca, Alberta, took a different route from either of the Ontario schools when it started its electronic MBA in 1994. It decided to go on-line, and relied on Lotus Notes, a specialized software package, as the medium of contact between students and professors. More recently, several specialized programs, such as Dalhousie's MBA in financial services, have also started to deliver a substantial part of their courses through distance methods.

The rapid growth of distance MBAs has stirred up some strong feelings among educators, with Athabasca being everyone's favorite whipping boy. Off the record, many business school deans disparage Athabasca's MBA, saying that the admission standards aren't as high or the material as rigorous as in a traditional program. Students, though, are flocking to the program. Based on the 640 students it enrolled for 1997-98, Athabasca claims to be the largest executive MBA program in Canada.

Queen's videoconferencing program also claims to be the largest executive MBA program in Canada, based on its record of graduating more students each year than anyone else. But other than in terms of raw numbers, it's difficult to compare Athabasca with Queen's or Western. Students in Athabasca's program file assignments and join in on-line discussions whenever it's convenient for them—if that happens to be 2 a.m. Wednesday or 11 p.m. Sunday, so be it. In contrast, students in both the Queen's and Western programs follow a schedule that requires them to be in class on consecutive Fridays and Saturdays every second week. Queen's and Western also require students to spend a couple of weeks on campus at the beginning of the program so they can get to know one another face-to-face before returning home to begin videoconferencing.

Both Queen's and Western have tried to maintain aspects of the traditional classroom. Walk into a videoconferencing site in either program and you'll see two regular-size TV screens at the front of the room. One TV shows the professor in London or Kingston. The other TV shows an electronic blackboard on which the professor can write down an equation or display a transparency. Other than the tele-visual aids, class is conducted in the usual B-school fashion, with the professor lecturing or asking questions, and students volunteering answers. When a student is speaking, his or her face fills the TV screen so that participants at other locations can see who is making a point.

The biggest difference between the two videoconferencing programs is Western professors can see eight monitors at once while Queen's professors can see only one. "A big hallmark of what we do in the case-study method is not so much giving people great wisdom as extracting ideas. We like to be able to see when students are putting up their hand tentatively and when they're jumping up and down with their hand in the air," says Terry Deutscher, director of Western's videoconferencing program.

Hands are invisible in Athabasca's program. Its curriculum is entirely print-based and is delivered over the Internet except for a week-long summer session and two weekend sessions that may be taken at any point in the program. The rest of the time students communicate with each other and with their professors through Lotus Notes.

While students in the videoconferencing programs take several classes concurrently—just as in a traditional MBA—Athabasca students work on one eight-week course at a time. Students read the course material on-line, then regroup into teams and discuss the case among themselves and with a "teacher coach." Students are evaluated on their participation, just as they would be in a regular MBA classroom, but the discussion doesn't happen in real time. Instead, students can log on whenever they feel like it, read the electronic messages that have already been posted, and add their own contribution.

Reach out and teach someone

Distance MBA programs use videoconferencing (Queen's and Western) or on-line "groupware" (Athabasca) to connect professors and students.

UNIVERSITY	Athabasca	Queen's	Western
Enrollment	640	314	117
Women	29%	26%	31%
Western Canada	57.7%	26.8%	48%
Central Canada (Ont and Que)	36.4%	68.5%	52%
Eastern Canada	3.1%	3.5%	none
International students	2.8%	1.3%	none

UNIVERSITY	Athabasca	Queen's	Western
Average age	40	38	39
Average years of work experience	9*	15	16
Minimum years of work experience	3*	8	8
Number of inquiries yearly	4,534	5,846	2,652
Average GMAT	not required	570	584
Average salary upon enrollment	$65,683	not tracked	$87,000
Average salary upon graduation	$76,579	not tracked	not tracked
Total number of grads	79	208	85
Enrollment cap	none	170 per year	60 per year
Tuition	$19,550	$57,000	$57,000

* Athabasca requires managerial experience

If you're not a convert to distance education, talking to people from Queen's or Athabasca can make you feel a bit as if you've wandered into a scene out of 1984. Just as George Orwell's characters were bombarded with the notion that War is Peace, enthusiasts for distance education insist that Distance is Closeness. Don Nightingale, director of Queen's executive MBA, argues that in a traditional classroom even people in the front row are three metres away from the prof and people in the back row may be as far away as 12 metres. But in videoconferencing, everyone is much closer to the prof's face on the screen. Professors and students in both programs insist that the interaction is better in these distance programs than in traditional classrooms. "I'm able to get a better conversation going in the videoconferencing format," says Michael Bennett who teaches finance and economics in the Queen's program. He believes that videoconferencing removes much of the fear from "cold calls"—the business school practice of calling on people without warning to analyze cases or answer a question—because he always throws out a question to a particular site, rather than to an individual student.

In Athabasca's case, students say that dealing solely with the written word means you get a higher quality response. People think before firing off an e-mail. One person can't dominate the conversation since, theoretically at least, there's no limit to the amount of airtime. "The conversation goes in all kinds of interesting directions. Some people may not log on for a couple of days and when they do the discussion can turn around," says Ron Edmonds, a professor in the program. In many ways, the program simulates the workplace, especially in areas such as business banking where large projects are often completed solely via e-mail communication. The downside? "You don't get the puzzled look [that you get in a regular classroom] that tells you you're not explaining things well," says Edmonds. Also, poor typing skills can really slow you down.

Queen's has polled students and found that those who have experience of both the videoconferencing MBA and the traditional live executive MBA in Ottawa prefer the electronic alternative. One advantage of the videoconferencing MBA is the cross-country perspective you get from other students. Another advantage: if you don't understand something the prof just said, you can turn to your teammates and get a quick explanation that doesn't interrupt the flow of the class the way it would in a traditional classroom.

Not everyone, though, is glowing in their praise of distance education. The people at Western, for instance, consider videoconferencing to be a serviceable but inferior alternative to a real classroom. The school relies heavily on the case-study method, which depends on rapid give-and-take between professors and students, and it believes even the best distance education is only an approximation of what goes on in a live forum. Western limits its program to 60 students a year because it wants its executive MBA classes to be as similar as possible to classes in the regular MBA and because it feels that you can't have an authentic case-study experience with a larger class. Ed Cloutier, the chief information officer of the Richard Ivey

School of Business at Western, is appalled at the thought of a professor not being able to see all students. "Students could go to lunch half an hour early, and the professor wouldn't know it," he says.

The reputation of distance education has not been enhanced by Athabasca's recent decision to stop requiring the GMAT for admission to its MBA program. Peter Carr, associate director of Athabasca's MBA program, says that the GMAT isn't relevant for students with extensive management experience. But while it's true the GMAT does tend to evaluate only a fairly narrow range of test-taking abilities and quantitative skills, it's hard to understand why a school would want to deprive itself of a piece of useful information with which to evaluate students. In 1995, the average score of Athabasca admittees was 566—not stellar but par for many regular MBA programs. By 1996, the average score had fallen to 535. (The average GMAT score in Western's and Queen's videoconferencing programs is 584 and 570, respectively.) One can't help wondering if Athabasca's average entering GMAT score has sunk even further with the admission of more and more students.

How Are Distance Grads Doing?

Since the first distance MBA grads have been on the market for only two years, it's difficult to assess how they are faring in the competition for jobs and salaries. Many grads do receive promotions while they're in the program or upon their graduation, says Queen's Don Nightingale. But the distance programs at Queen's and Western, like many executive MBA programs, deliberately eschew any attempts to place their grads with new employers since they don't want to damage relationships with the current employers who are paying their employees' tuition.

Athabasca is more open about who is moving where. It is establishing a database with names of recruiters who have approached them about grads. One of these is Lindy Arnold, a partner with the Glazin Group, an executive search firm based in Vancouver. While Arnold hasn't placed any Athabasca grads, she sees no reason to prefer students from a traditional program. "Both programs are going to produce people who have worked hard and have brushed shoulders with other bright people," she says. Furthermore, Arnold says, many employers are looking for precisely the kind of discipline and self-sacrifice that distance programs demand.

And how do students feel? Two years into her MBA, Royal Bank's Ritchie is delighted with Athabasca's program and has persuaded other people in her company to enroll. She recently returned from a holiday at the cottage with two more required courses under her belt. Her employer views an Athabasca MBA no differently from a traditional one. Ritchie hasn't learned anything earth-shattering so far, she says, just some of the academic jargon that she felt she was missing. "I knew most of the stuff already. I just didn't know I knew it."

CHAPTER FOUR

Co-op MBAs

BY DAVID BERMAN

The following article by David Berman, written when he was a staff writer with Canadian Business, appeared in the 1998 MBA issue.

Linda Burlison is only 25, but she has already had a taste of three high-profile business careers. She helped Ernst & Young Management Consulting analyze the nascent electronic commerce industry. She managed projects at Caught in the Web Inc., a small Toronto designer of Internet sites. And she tracked client data for mbanx, Bank of Montreal's electronic banking division—a job that allowed her to dine on occasion with the bank's top echelon of executives. "I spent two hours having lunch with the second-in-charge of the whole bank," she says. "And many people in the bank had never even seen him, let alone had lunch with him."

What's Burlison's secret for landing such plush jobs? She is a co-op student at the Michael G. DeGroote School of Business at McMaster University. The school requires its MBA students to mix four terms of school with three work terms of four months each. Burlison, a former Canadian senior champion in rhythmic gymnastics, had little in the way of corporate experience when she started the program and found the work experience a godsend. "What I've ended up with is a great job, in a great company, in a great industry," she says. "Each of the co-op terms has guided me toward both the industry that I want to work in and the role that I want in that industry."

No wonder co-op programs are bursting out all over the Canadian MBA scene. Most are designed for people like Burlison: students in their early 20s who lack work experience and aren't sure what line of business they want to pursue. The three schools in Canada that offer co-op MBA programs—McMaster, Université de Sherbrooke, and University of Windsor—believe classroom instruction becomes far more interesting if it can be immediately applied to the real world. At the very least, these schools figure that work terms give their students a chance to make valuable contacts as well as to find out what does—and doesn't—interest them as a future career.

> It's no coincidence that co-op schools lack the name-brand prestige of such venerable institutions as the Richard Ivey School of Business at the University of Western Ontario or the Joseph L. Rotman Centre for Management at the University of Toronto. When asked why Western hasn't gone the co-op route, the MBA program's director, Randy Kudar, chuckles. "We have students coming in with about five years of full-time work experience," he says. "So the concept of a co-op program probably isn't quite as relevant as it is to people who don't have any work experience."

The schools that are pushing co-op education see it as a way to circumvent their students' lack of experience—not to mention the downright snobbery that often works against them in the job market. "Employers wanted people with experience. That was the bottom line," says Dana Tonus, director of co-op education and career services at the University of Windsor, which made its MBA predominately co-op in 1996.

"Students who weren't graduating through co-op were having difficulty finding employment." Windsor—whose slogan is "No work experience, no problem!!"—has an 87% placement rate for its grads. Sherbrooke and McMaster boast a 100% placement rate after graduation.

If co-op education is a good deal for students, it can be a great deal for many employers. They gain the chance to put prospective employees through a prolonged testing period—and, if they don't like what they see, they can send their co-op students back to school without any obligation to hire them full-time. "We're always looking forward to how we're going to attract the brightest and the best, and this is really an avenue into that," says Sara Knapp, Bank of Montreal's director of capital at risk. This past spring, the bank hired 10 McMaster MBA graduates—most of them former co-op placements—on a permanent basis.

> But some employers have yet to come calling. In fact, if there is a knock against co-op MBA programs, it's their inability—as yet—to place their students with investment banks and top-tier management consultants. If you want to graduate into a six-figure job on Wall Street, look elsewhere. But if you're a relatively inexperienced 20-something who is seeking an opportunity to find your place in the business world, look no further.

How the Programs Stack Up

Co-op programs are available in a range of styles to fit your needs. Université de Sherbrooke, a French-only university, puts its 35 MBA students into the real world for only a single work term of 12 to 18 weeks. McMaster's 106-student program goes to the other end of the spectrum, insisting on a total of 12 months of work and 16 months of academic study. University of Windsor's program is somewhere in the middle, with two four-month work terms and 16 months of study.

Faculties of work
Canada's three major co-op MBA programs offer widely different experiences.

Michael G. DeGroote School of Business, McMaster University, Hamilton, Ont.

co-op enrollment: 106

average age: n/a

total length of program: 28 months

number of academic terms: 4

number of work terms: 3

duration of each work term: 4 months

major co-op employers: Bank of Montreal, Bank of Nova Scotia, Northern Telecom Ltd., Deloitte & Touche

placement rate upon graduation: 100%

average salary upon graduation:
    $51,030 (graduates without prior work experience)
    $62,200 (graduates who entered the program with one or more years of professional work experience)

University of Windsor, Windsor, Ont

co-op enrollment: 50

average age: 24

total length of program: 24 months

number of academic terms: 4

number of work terms: 2

duration of each work term: 4 months

major co-op employers: Northern Telecom Ltd., various

> banks, Ford Motor Co. of Canada Ltd., Bayer Inc. Canada
> placement rate upon graduation: 87%
> average salary upon graduation: $48,500
>
> **Université de Sherbrooke, Sherbrooke, Que.**
> co-op enrollment: 35
> average age: 33
> total length of program: 16 to 18 months
> number of academic terms: 3
> number of work terms: 1
> duration of each work term: 12 to 18 weeks
> major co-op employers: Pratt & Whitney Canada Inc., QuébecTel
> placement rate upon graduation: 100%
> average salary upon graduation: n/a

Other schools have injected a few co-op elements into their MBA programs. The Schulich School of Business at Toronto's York University offers an international MBA (or IMBA), which includes an internship in a foreign country. Students study one of six world regions and then hone in on one particular country. After a year at Schulich, students fan out to their chosen lands where they must work a minimum of 12 weeks, often at foreign offices of large Canadian-based companies.

> ### Schools offering work terms and internships
>
> If you're not interested in a full-blown co-op program, the following MBA programs have co-op-like features which will also allow you to get some hands-on experience with a company. These may be optional or compulsory and may last anywhere from five to twelve weeks. For further details, consult the profiles section of this book.
>
> British Columbia
> Dalhousie
> Laval
> Moncton
> New Brunswick—Fredericton
> New Brunswick—Saint John
> Ottawa
> Queen's
> Simon Fraser
> Victoria
> York

Whether co-op students work here or abroad, most of their work-term placements tend to be entry-level positions at mid-sized to large companies, ranging from consulting organizations to banks to established high-tech firms. The fledgling MBAs have considerable choice over where they end up: at McMaster, during last year's final term, there were three employers for every student—and students are also encouraged to seek out their own placements.

Once ensconced in their assignments, co-op students are usually treated the same as regular employees. They are often given a high level of responsibility. Hewlett-Packard (Canada) Ltd., the computer and electronics manufacturer based in

Mississauga, Ontario, has hired two MBA co-op students, each for a four-month work term. "They were working at a pretty high level," says John Cross, vice-president of human resources. "It was really hard to differentiate them from our full-time hires." One student worked in marketing, analyzing market segmentation and product sales for one of Hewlett-Packard's product managers. The other student worked as a financial analyst, examining a Hewlett-Packard product line and analyzing its expenses and projected targets.

At smaller companies, co-op students can actually take a big role in planning and developing strategy. "At Caught in the Web, they wanted to learn from us," says Bob Basadur, a McMaster student who spent a work term at the Internet designer. "I think they felt that they were getting business people fairly inexpensively, who could push their projects and give them a bit more thinking." Basadur, who still works at Caught in the Web part-time now that his work term is complete, drafts business plans to provide the company's sales force with the ammunition needed to close deals.

Most co-op employers are motivated by a mixture of impulses: philanthropy, the prospect of finding hot new talent, and the chance to benefit from the enthusiasm of young people who are desperate to prove themselves. "The students are definitely very keen," says Bank of Montreal's Sara Knapp. "You can sometimes become complacent with what you do, and they kind of inject this enthusiasm. When you're a student, anything is possible, and they've got this unbelievable work ethic."

Is a Co-op MBA for You?

But MBA co-ops are not for everyone. Students who have considerable work experience would likely find many of the work terms beneath them. Average weekly pay hovers in the $500 to $600 range. And students who already have a clear understanding of how they want to apply their MBA might find some of their work assignments, and the contacts that come with them, aren't helpful to their long-term career objectives.

The biggest downside to MBA co-ops, though, is that they simply do not give their students access to the top jobs. The average starting salary this past year for graduates of the MBA program at University of Toronto was an enviable $78,400—26% higher than McMaster's $62,200 (in the case of grads with some work experience), and 62% higher than Windsor's $48,500. When Bankers Trust came scouting for talent in Canada last year—the first year it has ever done so—U of T was the only business school on its list. And when Mercer Management Consulting Inc. goes shopping for Canadian MBA grads, it doesn't look at co-op schools, regardless of the schools' trial offers.

Admittedly, these jobs are in the uppermost tier. Most MBA grads, no matter what Canadian business school they're attending, would have a hard time gaining access to them. But, if you're on the hunt for a big paycheque immediately upon graduation, a co-op school may not be the best place for you.

Where co-op programs shine is in helping fresh-faced 20-somethings get their bearings in the business world. Linda Burlison, for one, doesn't regret her choice of school. After finishing her bachelor's degree, she won acceptance to U of T's prestigious MBA program—but declined the offer in favour of McMaster's co-op alternative. "If I had gone to U of T, what would I have ended up with?," she says. "I would probably still not know what I was going to do, and I would still not have very much work experience." For Burlison, who has fallen in love with the burgeoning Internet industry and plans to work at Caught in the Web full-time when she completes her MBA this December, the decision to take the co-op route couldn't have been smarter.

PART II

Business School Profiles

University of Alberta

The University of Alberta is an apt reflection of Edmonton, the city which it has called home since its founding in 1908. Edmonton is a government and research town rather than a corporate one, and no where is that more visible than in the business school. Government is regularly the largest employer of the MBA class. Says Dave Jobson, director of the MBA, "If you're looking for a client-based entrepreneurial program, go someplace else—go to Calgary, they've got a very downtown-oriented faculty."

The Faculty of Business at the University of Alberta has long been one of the more theoretical business schools around. Three professors hold prestigious 3M teaching fellowships; many more are assiduous writers of papers. The faculty is one of a select group of Canadian business schools that have been accredited by the American Assembly of Collegiate Schools of Business. "U of A has a very strong academic base," says an MBA student, adding, "they're so heavily academic that sometimes the teaching suffers. I think every academic will attest to the fact that they need to integrate themselves a bit better with the business community."

But curricula are gradually becoming more applied. The MBA program now has a mandatory business practicum and a mentor program that matches up Edmonton business people with MBA students. In 1995 the faculty started an Executive MBA program which it runs with the Faculty of Management at the University of California. It is also considering another partnership program, this one an MBA in resource management.

A-list Alumni

- Steven J. Glover MBA '87: Executive Director, Institute of Chartered Accountants of Alberta
- Gay Mitchell MBA '86: Executive Vice-President, Human Resources, Royal Bank of Canada
- Laurie Beattie MBA '86: Vice-President, Financial Reporting and Budgets, Consumers' Gas Co.
- Russell Kupin MBA '77: President, K-Five Energy Consulting Inc.
- Grant Devine MBA '70: Former Premier, Province of Saskatchewan

U of A has a large sprawling campus of 220 acres that seeps into the surrounding neighbourhood. There is a huge variety of building styles: graceful old buildings on quiet avenues, cement monsters, "the Butterdome," the ultra-modern sports complex that is bright yellow and shaped like a pound of butter. Many buildings are connected by hallways and students scurry through the connections in winter. Business is in a new building built in the late 1980s that is attached to Hub Mall, the large mall-cum-residence on campus.

MBA

Getting In

For entry in September 1998, the MBA program received 375 applications for full-time study; it accepted 90 of those for full-time study and 65 for part-time. You need a minimum average of B; the average grade of admitted students is a B+. As of 1997-98, work experience is a requirement, though 8% of the current enrollment came straight from an undergrad program into the MBA.

Atmospherics

The MBA at U of A attracts a diverse group of people. "You're dealing with a group of people who weren't attracted to places like Western. It's a more unique and entertaining fund of students," says one student. Students are high-school teachers, engineers, lawyers, artists. "I'm certainly the only person in the program with a home economics degree," points out another student. About 70% of students have work experience.

There are no two ways about it, if you choose this MBA, you will be either a poet or a quant—and Jobson will inform you of this during orientation. "Poets, rightfully so, get a little stressed out about having to deal with the use of numbers that they've never seen before in their life," says one self-described quant. This is certainly not to suggest that poets should stay away from this program. Any poet who can hack the number crunching in the core before scuttling off to human resources management, the traditional poetic refuge, will feel a deep sense of satisfaction. Most quants are full of solicitude for poets. The faculty is also extremely responsive to students, often asking for feedback and suggestions on how to improve the program. Jobson takes students to lunch to ask them how they like the program.

Profs, Programs, and Particulars

The U of A's two-year MBA program went through a review recently. One change is a redesigned core year. All introductory courses are now six weeks long and are taught in an integrated fashion. This allows students to get a taste of most functional areas in first semester. Despite initial hiccups, students like the shorter course format. Still the pace can be a bit of a jolt. August orientation is intended to bring students up to speed on subjects like financial mathematics, but as one student noted: "By the time finance rolled around, we had forgotten absolutely everything we learned in August." The MBA has also added skills instruction to the curriculum, mostly through a team-skills boot camp that starts off the year.

> The second big change is a variety of joint degrees and programs. There have been two joint programs for some time: an MBA/LLB and an MBA/Engineering. Now there are two more: an MBA/Master in forestry and an MBA/Master in agriculture. Specializations are available in leisure and sports management and international business. Two more were added in 1998: technology transfer, which deals with such things as start-ups in high-tech and intellectual property, and natural resources and energy. Both of these new areas have a summer internship requirement. "By adding these unique specializations, we hope we'll get students from Eastern Canada, who will come simply because they can do it here," says Jobson.

The MBA has been making itself more applied. The business practicum is done in teams over one semester. Students have done studies for the city of Edmonton, the Edmonton Symphony Orchestra, and Sherritt International Corp., among others. There is a mentor program that most students participate in, though mentors' levels of involvement vary. Jobson has also started a case competition for the MBA students.

Gradventures

- Chauvco Resources (Guy Turcotte MBA '76)
- Native Venture Capital Co. Ltd. (Milt Pahl MBA '71)

Living It Up

MBA students hang out in the MBA lounge in the business building. "We sit around and vent and can be ourselves there," says one. The social life revolves around three campus pubs: the Room at the Top, known universally as the RATT, on top of the Student Union Building, the Power Plant, and Dewey's ("incredibly smoke-filled"). One of the MBA students runs an Italian restaurant called Fiore's that became a hangout for the class of '97. (He recently switched to the part-time program, so the restaurant is likely to be a hot spot for some time yet.)

The three MBA student clubs are the MBA Association, the Volunteer Action Network, and the Varsity Consulting Group (VCG). Fifteen students work in the VCG providing consulting to Edmonton businesses. It is run by students in consultation with Ernst & Young.

The Payoff

MBA students are pleased with the Office of Placement Services but feel that the office could do more to reach out to the business community. "There is certainly the odd posting and employers do recruit, but it's more the employer approaching OoPS rather than OoPS taking a systematic approach," says one student. The office is geared more to undergrad students and to co-op than to the MBA, and only 19% of the MBA class found a job through OoPS. About 100 recruiters come on campus. The office reached 52 out of 60 grads of the class of '98 and found that 92% of them were employed within six months of graduation. The highest percentage of jobs were in government. Consulting was next, followed by financial/banking and oil and gas. Average starting salary was $63,913.

Executive MBA

In 1994 the business schools at the University of Alberta and the University of Calgary joined forces to work on their first co-operative endeavour. The result was the first Executive MBA in Alberta, which started in 1996. "Initially it's hard to get two institutions to co-operate," says Alan Conway, director of Calgary's half of the program. "But after the fact, you wonder why you had reservations."

> The EMBA targets managers with at least seven years of managerial experience; most students have between 15 and 20.

For two years students are in class every two weeks on Friday and Saturday from early August to late May. Virtually all classes are held in Calgary, and students who live in Edmonton commute to class every two weeks. One week-long session on business-government relations is held in Edmonton. Teaching is shared equally between the two institutions. At the moment, there are twice as many U of C students, but if U of A enrollment increases substantially, more classes will be given in Edmonton.

The program covers the basics of a standard MBA. "We wanted grads of this program to be held accountable to the same type of knowledge as regular MBAs," says Conway. Most of the core material is integrated across functional areas. First year has a couple of projects embedded in different courses where participants work within their organization. There is one elective in second year and an optional international trip that has sent students to Prague, Vienna, and Budapest.

The Bottom Line

Foreign Affairs

The faculty has 17 agreements with universities in Austria, Chile, Denmark, Finland, France, Germany, Hong Kong, Japan, Mexico, Sweden, Thailand, and Scotland.

Money for Nothing

MBA students are eligible for seven scholarships, ranging in value from $600 to $2,500. In 1996, 11 students were employed as research or teaching assistants.

Other Options

- Joint MBA/LLB
- Joint MBA/Eng.
- Joint MBA/Master in agriculture
- Joint MBA/Master in forestry
- PhD

Contacts

Faculty of Business • University of Alberta • Edmonton, AB • T6G 2R6 • (403) 492-5693 • www.bus.ualberta.ca

UNIVERSITY OF ALBERTA—VITAL STATISTICS

total university enrollment	29,863
total full-time undergrad enrollment	25,264
number of full-time professors in the faculty of business	64
number of part-time professors	76
number of women professors	6 full-time; 17 part-time
MBA	
full-time enrollment	130
part-time enrollment	200
size of entering class	65 full-time; 55 part-time
women students	33%
out-of-province students	40%

international students	15%
students straight from undergrad	8%
average age	28
annual tuition	$4,400
annual tuition for international students	$8,300
length of program	2 years
number of applications	375
number of acceptances	N/A
cut-off grade for admission	B
average grade of admittees	B+
average GMAT	610
years of work experience required	2
average years of work experience	4.5
size of core classes	65
size of electives	20
classes taught by full-time faculty	95%
grads employed within six months of graduation	92%
number of on-campus recruiters	100
grads hired through placement office	19%
average starting salary	$63,913
what employment figures are based on	52 out of 60 grads of the class of 1998

Executive MBA

enrollment	71
women students	20%
average age	40
average GMAT	585
years of work experience required	7
average years of work experience	15 to 20
cost of program	$40,000

Athabasca University

The medium is the message at Athabasca University, the principal distance education school in Canada. Athabasca even offers a Master's degree in distance ed, which is, naturally, delivered via distance ed. So it was hardly surprising that when the university added to its graduate programs in business, it started an MBA in information technology delivered electronically.

Athabasca has been in business for nearly 30 years now, providing education to students all over Canada, and even some abroad, who might otherwise not have access to a university. These students juggle jobs and family and take courses electronically, by correspondence, through videoconferencing, or live.

In 1994, the Centre for Innovative Management, an independent business unit at Athabasca that is run without government funds, was founded to create and manage two graduate programs in business management that are delivered electronically: an advanced graduate diploma in management and an executive style MBA that, with more than 600 students, is the largest and fastest growing MBA in Canada. Since that time, two other MBA programs have started, the aforementioned MBA in information technology in 1999 and, in 1997, an MBA in agriculture that is offered in joint partnership with Guelph.

MBA

Getting In

The MBA received 444 applications in 1997-98 and accepted 312. Students can enter the program in September, January, or May. There is no minimum required average. Recently, the program has also stopped requiring the GMAT (in the last year that they used it, the average was 535). Everyone must have at least three years of managerial experience; the average is nine years. About 20% of students don't have an undergraduate degree or a professional designation; to compensate they must have at least ten years of managerial experience and are admitted provisionally to the graduate diploma—essentially the first half of the MBA. Most diploma students then upgrade to the MBA.

> You can't do the program without a computer, 486 or better—Pentium is recommended. The program provides the Lotus Notes software, course packages, and multimedia materials. "We give them all the material to study on a desert island, provided they have a communications link," says Dwight Thomas, former MBA program director. Alas, Macintosh users must look elsewhere: the MBA does not accommodate these enthusiasts.

Atmospherics

Total flexibility is the hallmark of the program. If you're the type of person who likes to wake up at 5 a.m., work for two hours, go to your day job, and work a little bit more while dinner is cooking, this is the program for you. The program also gives you something of a national perspective: 34% of students are from Alberta, 35% from Ontario, and the remainder from assorted provinces and territories. There are a few international students.

Most interaction between students takes place through e-mail in group discussions and on team assignments, but not in real time, since Lotus Notes doesn't have chat rooms in cyberspace. Dealing solely with the printed word can be refreshing. "People think about what they're writing. You usually get a high quality response," says a human resources specialist from the first MBA intake in 1994. When classmates send annoying messages, you can simply not read them or at least cool down before responding. People will also call each other up about assignments.

In addition to the electronic courses, there are two weekend schools and a week-long summer school that all students must attend. Three summer sessions were held in 1998: in Hamilton, Calgary, and Regina.

Students say that technical support is good and that the faculty is responsive. There are graduate student advisers available to answer questions about assignments.

Profs, Programs, and Particulars

The MBA focuses less on functional areas, such as accounting, marketing, and so forth, than on strategic management. "Those kinds of skills are going to be far more easily applied. I definitely think more in terms of strategy, weakness, and risk now," says an MBA who started the program in 1995.

The program is in three phases. The first two phases are required courses with a comprehensive exam at the end of each phase. The last phase includes electives and an applied project. Electives vary from semester to semester. Some past topics are total quality management, advanced project management, and enterprise for small business.

Each weekend and summer-school session has a theme. One session might deal with leadership, another with management of change. Students also have participated in a management game simulation. "It's more like a business workshop than a university classroom," says one student.

In addition to the handful of full-time professors, the program makes use of about 50 virtual faculty members drawn from universities across Canada, the US, and the UK. This year the MBA even held a conference for its virtual faculty, with sessions on such topics as how to evaluate student participation in on-line courses.

The Payoff

All students are employed full time while in the program. The first MBAs graduated from the program in 1997 and administrators are starting to develop a database in order to track grads.

MBA in Agriculture

In September 1997 the first cohort of 32 students entered Athabasca's MBA in agriculture, offered jointly with the University of Guelph. Students spend the first half of the program taking Athabasca courses and completing the Graduate Diploma in Management. They then transfer to Guelph where the remainder of their courses are on-line agriculture courses. Students will likely complete the degree in about three years.

The Bottom Line

Money for Nothing

The MBA program does not offer any scholarships.

Contacts

Centre for Innovative Management • Athabasca University • 301 Grandin Park Plaza • 22 Sir Winston Churchill Ave. • St. Albert, AB • T8N 1B4 • (800) 561-4650 or (403) 459-1144 • www.athabascau.ca/mba/index.html

ATHABASCA UNIVERSITY—VITAL STATISTICS

MBA

enrollment	640
women students	29%
Alberta students	34%
Ontario students	35%
other Canadian students	32%
international students	1%
students straight from undergrad	none
average age	40
total tuition	$19,550
total tuition for international students	US$19,550
estimated total cost of phone charges	$1,500
number of applications	444
number of acceptances	312
cut-off grade for admission	none
average grade for admittees	N/A
average GMAT	N/A
years of work experience required	3
average years of work experience	9
number of full-time professors	6
number of part-time professors	45
number of women professors	3 full-time; 7 part-time

MBA in Agriculture

enrollment	60
size of entering class	30
women students	25%
international students	2
students straight from undergrad	none

average age	43
total tuition	$21,500
total tuition for international students	$25,000
length of program	30 months
number of applications	65
number of acceptances	30
cut-off grade for admission	75%
average grade of admittees	75%
average GMAT	not required
years of work experience required	3 to 10
average years of work experience	8
size of core classes	30
size of electives	15
classes taught by full-time faculty	80%

University of British Columbia

It seems fitting that vast geographical distances should separate the University of Western Ontario from the University of British Columbia, since business schools in Canada tend to situate themselves somewhere on an imaginary line between the two. If people see Western as the prototype for the prestigious case study school, they see UBC as the prototype for the prestigious research school. Ask UBC profs about the case study method, and chances are they'll sound a bit dubious.

> Says Michael Goldberg, former dean of the Faculty of Commerce and Administration at UBC, "We feel that theories have very long half-lives and that they're very valuable to somebody over their career. A more practical approach is actually impractical, because if you give people skills that relate to the current business scene, the world changes and you haven't equipped them with the theories that allow them to go back and say, 'Gee, I have to get back to first principles.'" So if you're considering an MBA at this academic powerhouse, remember that theory is likely to infuse a good part of what you do.

But even UBC has moved to respond to complaints that MBA programs turn out students who are stuffed full of theory and little else. In 1995 the faculty inaugurated a modular 15-month MBA program that has a team-taught integrated core, specializations, an internship, and a substantial professional development component—radical stuff for a school that never met a number it didn't like. To make sure the professors buy in, Goldberg made it a privilege to teach in the core and allotted more teaching credit to the core than to regular courses. In January 1999, a new MBA in Financial Services with substantial input from industry started in cooperation with Simon Fraser's Faculty of Business Administration.

Within the province, UBC is the most prestigious university. It has been around since 1908 and the business school is the oldest in BC. But as the only top business school west of Ontario, the faculty seems slightly anxious about what goes on beyond the Rockies. When asked about any weaknesses in the revamped MBA, more than one UBC administrator says right off, "the fact that the media doesn't cover it."

> UBC is an excellent place for students interested in international business, especially the Asia Pacific economies. There is an extensive selection of exchange programs and the faculty also hosts about 70 exchange students from abroad annually. The faculty's executive development branch has several residential programs that bring in Korean managers for a mix of English language, intercultural training, and business training. More than 500 Korean business people have passed through UBC since 1994.

UBC's natural setting is stunning. The campus is on a promontory, with the ocean on one side and wooded endowment lands on the other. Campus buildings are less beautiful: most are concrete and box-like. The faculty has its own building. UBC is about 10 kilometres from downtown Vancouver.

MBA

Getting In

In September 1998, UBC enrolled the fourth class of its new MBA. For entry in 1998 the program received 607 applications and made 228 offers. A four-year undergraduate degree with a minimum standing of B+ is required. Two to three years of work experience are preferred, and all members of the entering class of 1998 had at least that. If there is still room in the class after students with high grades, high GMATs, and work experience have been admitted, the most important factor in evaluating additional candidates is work experience.

Atmospherics

The new MBA program attracts a different group of people from the old, many of whom say they would not have considered attending the old program. These students are generally older, with more work experience. "The class was chosen for its diversity. There are people of all backgrounds and all ages. It's just fascinating to see what they've done," says an MBA student. The class is slightly less diverse racially, says a recent grad from the old program, who comments: "Our first reaction was, God, it's so white!"

This program is intense. Goldberg estimates that even though the new program is nine months shorter, it has 4% more material than the old one. "We feel that in a 15-month period, you can work flat out," he says. Students get five weeks of holidays over the 15 months.

Students praise the interaction with the professors, especially those in the core. "They're colleagues more than teachers, and that's more of a professional environment," says one MBA student. The responsiveness of the faculty has made the inevitable glitches of a new program bearable.

Profs, Programs, and Particulars

The unofficial start of the program is the three-week August pre-core that allows students to brush up on basic areas and get used to sitting in a classroom again. Students aren't required to attend, but about two-thirds do. "One of the big advantages was that I was able to get to know almost two-thirds of my classmates before we got into anything really serious," says a student.

Core—or "learning about the firm," as Goldberg calls it—takes up all of first semester. Students go in as one cohort and are taught by the same six professors. All the functional areas are integrated, meaning that accounting, finance, and marketing, for instance, are taught as an integral part of understanding how the firm works, rather than just on their own merit. The teamwork of students is mirrored by the teamwork of the professors who are all in the classroom together. "You definitely get a higher level of performance from a professor that's being watched by his peers," a student says. The class works with one company over the semester that has agreed to be a showcase company for the core.

Six weeks of professional development are scattered throughout the program. Each week has an overall theme and each day of the week focuses on a different topic. Topics might be anything from current business events to teamwork or career-planning. During that week, the CEO Speaker Series brings in a CEO for an informal talk.

Once the core is done, students take their specialization modules—six-week courses that are taken four at a time. Unlike many shorter programs, this MBA manages to offer students an excellent selection of courses—more than 90 in total. On the downside, some of the students in the old MBA who have experienced both the old courses and the new say that these modules contain too much material. "It's a good idea in theory, but I found that they were taking all of the material from the 13-week courses and putting it into these six-week modules. Students were having to do too much reading," says a part-timer from the old MBA program.

> There are specializations in strategic management, information technology management, finance, and marketing and supply chain management. Finance and information technology are traditional strengths. "Profs are publishing papers and you're learning exactly what issues they're dealing with currently in their research," a student says.

The last part of the program is reserved for the 10- to 12-week internship and international exchanges. The internship is expected to match the specialization and can take several forms. A student might work as a security analyst, engage in a shadowing exercise, or prepare a feasibility study.

Living It Up

MBAs hang out in the faculty's Peter Lusztig lounge. Korners is the well frequented UBC grad pub. There are usually some students to be found in the Bird Coop, the weight room in the gym. Off campus, students head to Kitsilano, a Vancouver neighbourhood that has a lot of restaurants and bars. There are all kinds of outdoor activities for students to engage in.

The Commerce Graduate Society (CGS) runs numerous events, such as the Chinese New Year Banquet, which attracts students, alumni, and people from the business community, and the Bon Voyage Beach Barbecue. The CGS also co-ordinates the BC Business Awards.

The Payoff

Students get substantial career counselling during the professional development sessions of the curriculum. In addition, the Commerce Career Centre runs seminars on résumé writing and interviewing skills.

The CCC surveyed 94% of the class of '98 and found that within six months of finishing the program, 90% of respondents had found employment. Nearly half the grads

(49%) remained in the Greater Vancouver Area; 22% went to Ontario, mainly Toronto; 16% found jobs internationally; 2% went to the US, and 9% to other provinces in Canada. There were 139 companies recruiting on-campus for the class of 1997. Average base starting salary is $60,200, with salaries ranging from $40,000 to $104,000. Thirty-two percent of students found jobs through the Career Centre, while 21% found jobs that were directly related to their internship.

A-list Alumni

- Egizio Bianchini MBA '85: Vice-President, Nesbitt Burns Ltd.
- Robert Smith MBA '84: President and CEO, Seaboard Life Insurance Co.
- Kathryn Gallagher Morton MBA '83: President, Avonlea Traditions Inc.; President and Owner, Mascot Custom Character Products Inc.
- Bruce Birmingham MBA '71: President, The Bank of Nova Scotia
- Jean Pierre Soublière MBA '71: Chairman, SHL Systemhouse

MBA in Financial Services

The new MBA in Financial Services started in January 1999 with a cohort of 50. The program is a joint venture between the business schools of Simon Fraser University and the University of British Columbia, the most substantial cooperation between the two schools thus far. The program, which is entirely part-time, targets those employed in financial institutions such as banks, insurance companies, and credit unions, though students need not be employed in the sector to apply to the program. A consortium of 12 or so companies are involved in the MBA: as an advisory body, for case study and research sites, and for employment opportunities. There are two streams: a management of financial services organizations stream and a certification stream, in which students take courses that will enable them to graduate with both an MBA and a designation from an organization such as the Institute of Canadian Bankers or the Society for Management Accountants. The program is provisionally priced at about $20,000.

The Bottom Line

Foreign Affairs

The faculty has about 35 exchange agreements with universities in 19 countries in Asia, Australia, Europe, the Middle East, and South America.

Money for Nothing

There are 55 scholarships earmarked for MBA students. They range in value from $275 to $15,000. Graders earn $22.12 an hour for essay and other subjective marking, $10.59 an hour for test and other objective marking.

Other Options

- Joint MBA/LLB
- Master of Engineering in Advanced Technology Management
- Master of Science in Business Administration
- PhD

Contacts

Faculty of Commerce and Business Administration • University of British Columbia • 2053 Main Mall • Vancouver, BC • V6T 1Z2 • (604) 822-2211 • www.commerce.ubc.ca

UNIVERSITY OF BRITISH COLUMBIA—VITAL STATISTICS

total university enrollment	33,197
total full-time undergrad enrollment	19,814
number of full-time professors in the faculty of commerce and administration	87
number of part-time professors	12
number of women professors	8 full-time

MBA

full-time enrollment	185
part-time enrollment	25
size of entering class	95 full-time
women students	32%
out-of-province students	25%
international students	20%
students straight from undergrad	none
average age	29
total tuition and fees	$7,000
total tuition and fees for international students	$20,000
length of program	15 months
number of applications	607
number of acceptances	228
cut-off grade for admission	B+
average grade of admittees	N/A
average GMAT	618
years of work experience required	2 to 3 preferred
average years of work experience	4

size of core classes	100
size of electives	10 to 35
classes taught by full-time faculty	94%
grads employed within six months of graduation	90%
number of on-campus recruiters	139
grads hired through placement office	32%
average starting salary	$60,200
what employment figures are based on	94% of the class of '98

University of Calgary

Calgary and Edmonton have competing personalities, sports teams, and annual celebrations. Will they now compete over business schools? "Not yet, but we think that'll soon change," predicts a Calgary business student.

> The recently revamped MBA in Enterprise Development is the only MBA in Canada that can claim to be a factory for entrepreneurs. Thirty-seven percent of students from the first entering class started their own businesses. In its 1998 ranking of Canadian MBA programs with entrepreneurship content, the international *Journal of Business Venturing* ranked Calgary's MBA No. 1. The faculty is also one of four business schools in Canada that is accredited by the American Assembly of Collegiate Schools of Business (AACSB).

Founded in 1966, the University of Calgary is a young university with an ambitious Faculty of Management. Since the late '70s, when a group of influential Calgary business people began working to attract more resources to the faculty, the school has benefitted from considerable financial support from the community. The most tangible evidence of this support is Scurfield Hall, a building so splendid it has been dubbed "the temple of greed" by students in other faculties (with, need one say it, much less splendid facilities). Every door in Scurfield is embellished with a corporate donor plaque. But the help isn't only monetary: the school regularly solicits advice on its programs, and business people often show up at faculty events, such as the Friday morning faculty series, which features mini-seminars on topics such as change management.

Alas, U of C is not known for its beauty. "We do have more than one tree," a student points out. Many of the buildings are large, off-white, and concrete. The temple of greed is off in one corner of the campus. It's an airy light-filled building that throngs all day with students and business people. Scurfield has its own stock ticker, a relic of the Toronto Stock Exchange's pre-computerized days. It sits in the lobby and students post notes to each other on it.

MBA

Getting In

In 1997-98 the MBA received 293 applications and accepted 118 of those. The minimum grade for admission is 3.0 out of 4.0; the average grade of admitted students is 3.2. The MBA requires students to have at least three years' work experience. The admissions office doesn't screen students for entrepreneurial verve, but there is starting to be a fair amount of self-selection.

Atmospherics

U of C's MBA program attracts an older crowd—the average age of students is 33—that wants to do something different.

> "If I were 24 and wanted to work for GM, I probably would have gone to Harvard or Western," says a 40-year-old student who sold a thriving dental practice to enroll in the program. "A lot of the students aren't here because the MBA will make them a pile of money," he adds. "Everyone has an idea of what they want to do. No one comes into the program to find themselves," says a part-time MBA student.

Of course not everyone wants to start a company. "The program gives you an opportunity to work in the real world if you want to be a consultant," says a second-year MBA student from Russia who chose the program for its proximity to the oil industry. And some students just feel lucky to have a high-quality MBA program in their home town.

Students say the faculty is in touch with the students. "It just seemed like any time you wanted to they were more than willing to sit down and talk to you," says one alum. "When I was in dentistry, the profs were not on your side. But here I identified pretty early on, yeah, these guys are here to help us," adds another. In a new venture development course, it's quite likely that a professor will come in and talk about difficulties he's having running his own company.

Profs, Programs, and Particulars

Students go through first year as a cohort. Nine professors teach the core which is integrated across functional areas. The core faculty meet every second week to review the progress of the core. Alongside these intro courses, students participate in Clinic, which pairs up teams of students with an owner-managed company that has a growth plan. Clinic acts as a laboratory for the core, since students are acting as consultants to companies that face a wide spectrum of problems.

> **Gradventures**
>
> Bagelicious—a Calgary bagel franchise that makes bagels in as many flavours as Baskin Robbins makes ice cream (founded by part-timers Grant Oh and Darren Sjeld)

In second year, students may specialize in accounting, international business, management information systems, management of human resources, management of financial resources, management of public institutions, marketing and distribution systems, operations management, project management, or tourism management. But it's fair to say that specializations are almost secondary to the overarching entrepreneurial theme. Clinic continues into second year, and students are doing increasingly sophisticated consulting work with various companies. A number of students also begin working on their own start-ups during this year.

> Start-ups aren't the sole goal of the MBA in enterprise development. "What we're trying to do is set students up so they can either launch their own business as an outcome of the program, take a senior position in a growth company, or go into an existing company with a new venture orientation," says Alan Conway, director of the MBA.

So how does all this help you start your own company? "I don't think anyone is born an entrepreneur. But this program lets you think and reflect and plan so you can act like one," says a student who started his own bagel-making company with a classmate midway through the program. "In a case study you don't get to talk to the person who runs the business. Here there are no question marks. You figure out why he does it and you ask him." Adds an alum: "It really prepares you for what to look for. Half the problem with starting a business is being cornered and not knowing what's going to come up behind you." Students say that most of the profs have bought into the entrepreneurial orientation of the program.

Living It Up

Many students from out of province end up staying in Calgary after graduation because the city is so agreeable. Skiing is close by. Students will sometimes go mountain-biking during a two-hour break between classes.

The main hangout is the grad lounge in Scurfield Hall. Mescalero's for dinner and dancing is a popular off-campus place.

The MBA Association is the only club for MBA students. It organizes social events, such as Thank God It's Friday sessions, and co-ordinates students' involvement with various charities in the city. Several MBA students recently set up a small business consulting group.

The Payoff

Warning: starting your own business delays graduation. Thirty-seven percent of the students that entered the MBA in 1992 started a business, but if you look at the members of that class that actually graduated, the entrepreneur figure goes down to 12%. People will often move to the part-time program in order to devote themselves to their business.

In 1996-97, 776 companies recruited for commerce and MBA students. This represented 787 vacancies for MBA students. The Career Development Office (CDO) contacted 61 out of 92 grads of the class of 1997 and found that 78% had secured full-time positions; 15% were working in contract positions; and 7% had found part-time jobs. The average starting salary was $61,043.

> **A-list Alumni**
>
> - Stephen R. Sanford MBA '93: Senior Counsel and Secretary, Fluor Daniel Canada Inc.
> - Hal Kvisle MBA '82: President, Fletcher Challenge Petroleum Inc.
> - Charlie Fischer MBA '82: Senior Vice-President, Exploration and Production North America, Canadian Occidental Petroleum Inc.

The CDO goes into MBA classes and runs seminars during Clinic on dealing with executive search firms and using the Internet to look for work. Students are pleased with the office, but says one, "At the end of two years, they still did not know I had a science degree. What they should do is get to know the students better."

Executive MBA

In 1994 the business schools at the University of Alberta and the University of Calgary joined forces to work on their first co-operative endeavour. The result was the first Executive MBA in Alberta, which started in 1996. "Initially it's hard to get two institutions to co-operate," says Conway who directs Calgary's half of the EMBA. "But after the fact, you wonder why you had reservations."

> The EMBA targets managers with at least seven years of managerial experience; most students have between 15 and 20.

For two years students are in class every two weeks on Friday and Saturday from early August to late May. Virtually all classes are held in Calgary, and students who live in

Edmonton commute to class every two weeks. One week-long session on business-government relations is held in Edmonton. Teaching is shared equally between the two institutions. At the moment, there are twice as many U of C students, but if U of A enrollment increases substantially, more classes will be given in Edmonton.

The program covers the basics of a standard MBA. "We wanted grads of this program to be held accountable to the same type of knowledge as regular MBAs," says Conway. Most of the core material is integrated across functional areas. First year has a couple of projects embedded in different courses where participants work within their organization. There is one elective in second year and an optional international trip that has sent students to Prague, Vienna, and Budapest.

The Bottom Line

What the Judges Think

- 1996 MBA International Case Competition (MBAICC) at Concordia: 3rd place
- 1995 MBAICC: 1st place
- 1994 MBAICC: 1st place

Foreign Affairs

The faculty has agreements with the State Academy of Management in Russia; Uppsala University in Sweden; the University of Manchester Institute of Science and Technology in England; the University of Strathclyde in Scotland; the University of Texas at San Antonio in the US; and James Cook University in Australia.

Money for Nothing

There are 11 scholarships earmarked for MBA students. They are worth between $1,000 and $3,000.

Other Options

- MBA with thesis option, a program that is essentially a master of science in management
- PhD

Contacts

Faculty of Management • University of Calgary • 2500 University Drive N.W. • Calgary, AB • T2N 1N4 • (403) 220-5685 • www.ucalgary.ca/UofC/faculties/MGMT/index.html

UNIVERSITY OF CALGARY—VITAL STATISTICS

total university enrollment	23,737
total full-time undergrad enrollment	17,438
number of full-time professors in the faculty of management	84
number of part-time professors	30
number of women professors	22 full-time and part-time

MBA

full-time enrollment	106
part-time enrollment	249
size of entering class	66 full-time; 52 part-time
women students	45%
out-of-province students	25%
international students	10%
students straight from undergrad	none
average age	33
tuition	$454 per course
tuition for international students	$908 per course

length of program	2 years
number of applications	293
number of acceptances	118
cut-off grade for admission	3.0 out of 4.0
average grade of admittees	3.2
average GMAT	595
years of work experience required	3
average years of work experience	8
size of core classes	50 to 60
size of electives	25 to 40
classes taught by full-time faculty	100%
grads employed full-time within six months of graduation	94%
number of recruiters	776 for B.Comm and MBA
grads hired through placement office	N/A
average starting salary	$61,042
what employment figures are based on	61 out of 92 grads of the class of '97

Executive MBA

enrollment	71
women students	20%
average age	40
average GMAT	585
years of work experience required	7
average years of work experience	15 to 20
cost of program	$40,000

Concordia University

An administrator at Concordia's Faculty of Commerce and Administration provides the following summary: "McGill has the law school, the medical school, and Henry Mintzberg. We have everything else." Including a slight inferiority complex.

Concordia University is in Montreal, just minutes from famed McGill. "It's almost fun to be in second place. You push yourselves more," says Alan Hochstein, former director of Concordia's MBA program, who acknowledges that "competition is an emotional issue but not a practical one. We're fighting against a ghost." Indeed lots of students automatically choose McGill over Concordia. But plenty of others select Concordia first. There's no question that McGill has greater recognition beyond the confines of Quebec, but to many students that simply isn't an issue.

So what does Concordia have? It has an MBA that attracts many part-time students who are working professionals and one of two Executive MBAs in Montreal that enrolls as many francophone students as anglos.

> Concordia also offers a unique Aviation MBA that is supported by the International Air Transport Association and draws more than 95% of its participants from abroad.

In 1997 Concordia was accredited by the American Assembly of Collegiate Schools of Business. On the student activity side, Concordia hosts the yearly Concordia International Case Competition, one of the best known MBA case competitions. "It's a chance for a lot of senior executives to see something that Concordia MBA does and does well," says an MBA student.

Concordia is primarily a local institution but its roots run deep. The university was established in 1974. It is the result of a merger of two venerable Montreal institutions, Loyola College and Sir George Williams University, an institution that developed out of courses offered by Canada's first YMCA to working people who couldn't afford full-time schooling at other universities. Accessibility to education is still a key issue.

> The university has an enormous part-time population and "relative to McGill and the École des Hautes Études Commerciales, we probably have an open-door policy," says an administrator. This said, "it's easier to get in, but it's as hard or harder to get out."

While Concordia draws few international students compared with McGill, it tends to be more representative of the ethnic diversity of Montreal. Profs, on the other hand, are an international lot: 25 different ethnic groups and 30 different languages are represented in the faculty.

Concordia's rather dreary Sir George campus in downtown Montreal isn't much to speak of. Almost everything seems to be in the Hall Building, a big square building with miles of escalators conveying students from one floor to the next. The business building is in a dowdy office building down the street but there are ongoing plans to build a new facility on a recently purchased plot of land.

MBA

Getting In

The MBA received 497 applications in 1997-98 of which it accepted 175. There is no automatic GPA cut-off. The average grade of admitted applicants was 3.0 out of 4.3. You need a minimum of two years' work experience and most students have about six years' experience.

Atmospherics

Concordia MBAs are a diverse group of people. Most don't have an undergrad degree in business. "It's a more mature program, which was a concern because I had been out of school for a number of years," says a student. About 35% of students are francophone Montrealers, and almost two-thirds of students study part time.

The program aims to be customer oriented. There have been proposals to offer certain courses as early as 7:30 in the morning to accommodate student schedules. It's easy to switch between the part-time and full-time programs. "Students tell me they came to Concordia because the receptionist was polite to them on the phone," says Hochstein. "Everything stops here when a student comes in."

Profs, Programs, and Particulars

Concordia's MBA is a generalist program for people from other fields who want to acquire business skills. Because of this orientation, the core of the program takes about one-and-a-half years to complete, with one semester left for electives. Most don't mind the lack of choice. "Stats and accounting was stuff I haven't taken before," says one student. Another remarks: "The courses build on each other. I wouldn't want too much choice; I wouldn't know what to take."

Before the program starts, students who lack skills in math and computing must complete three commerce courses in these areas. One of the newest elements of the MBA are three managerial skills modules that are taken throughout the core. They cover such topics as time management, self-assessment, conflict resolution, and interviewing skills.

In their second year, students may choose between the MBA research project with four electives or the MBA practicum project with five electives. The practicum is spread out over two terms and requires students to go into a firm, talk to the principals, and write a report. Running the International Case Competition can replace the research project and the practicum. About 20 students are accepted into the case competition course and at the end of the course, three students are chosen to make up the organizing team.

> Strong functional areas are finance, management, and accounting. Human resources isn't as strong because of the lack of courses. "I'd love to have about five more HR courses," says one student.

Hochstein estimates that about 60% of classes are taught in lecture format, 35% in case study, and the remainder through other methods. Professors get high marks for teaching. Students have particular praise for the part-time faculty who have extensive experience in industry. But, adds a student: "Since Concordia doesn't have the name, they have to work harder. They need more contact with the business community."

Living It Up

MBAs hang out in the graduate student lounge in the building. The only real off-campus spot is Caesar's Pub, around the corner from the faculty. "The program is very part-time oriented. A lot of people go to class and go home," says one student.

The Commerce Graduate Students Association represents MBAs at Concordia. It runs a tutorial service for students who need help with course material. The Small Business Consulting Bureau provides advice to local small and medium-sized businesses. The annual Women and Work Symposium is a 26-year-old student-run conference that recruits prominent women from the business world to give talks. The yearly case competition also requires lots of volunteers.

The Payoff

Career placement for MBAs is vastly improved from two years ago, when the centre had one person who worked three days a week. This person, naturally, had little time to spend on bringing recruiters to campus. MBAs are now served by a new placement centre within the business school with three full-time staff. The director is working on attracting Toronto and New York investment banks and more consulting and marketing companies. The centre does not yet have any firm employment statistics but managed to chat with about half the MBA graduating class as they strode off the stage at graduation. This ad hoc survey showed that the average base starting salary was about $50,000 with a range between $38,000 to $120,000.

A-list Alumni

- Mutsumi Takahashi MBA '95: Newscaster and Writer, CFCF Inc.
- Robert Cariglia MBA '87: President, Freightliners Canada Inc.
- Andrew Ferrier MBA '83: President, Redpath Sugars
- Dave Goldman MBA '80: President and CEO, Noranda Metallurgy Inc.
- Humberto Santos MBA '79: Former President and CEO, Desjardins Laurentian Financial Corp.

Aviation MBA

The Aviation MBA, in the aviation capital of the world, is the only program of its kind. It was founded in 1991 when the International Air Transport Association (IATA) decided to start a program to train people in the industry.

Participants must have at least three years of experience in aviation and currently be employed in the industry. Most students have closer to eight years of experience. In the first years of the program, participants were restricted to airline employees, but students now come from airport and civil aviation authorities. There's the odd pilot in the program as well.

> The Aviation MBA is easily the most international of executive degrees in Canada: 96% of participants come from abroad and the program is marketed globally in Web pages, videos, trade journals, and at airport authority meetings. (The EMBA facilities even include a prayer room for Muslim students, complete with prayer mats and copies of the Koran.)

The program recently went to a one-year format with classes divided into four semesters. The curriculum covers the fundamentals of the regular MBA, while sessions at the end address specific issues such as airline marketing or yield management (making sure your seats get filled). A major part of the program is the project. Topics have ranged from the effects of deregulation to a study of in-flight personnel.

Material from the industry is brought in through case studies—though there's still a shortage of aviation cases. Simulation models, where students are divided into teams of five airlines, are also used. A distinguished speakers series brings in top airport and airline CEOs.

Many of the professors are regular Concordia faculty, but the AMBA also flies in profs from other universities.

Executive MBA

Concordia's EMBA started in 1985. It now enrolls about 59 people, mainly from Montreal and surrounding areas. More than half the people in the program are francophones. "The majority of people are functionally bilingual. Language is a non-issue; this is one of the more cherished characteristics of the program," says former director Kamal Argheyd. In fact, the program's main competitor is Université de Sherbrooke's French-language EMBA, which is held in the Montreal suburb of Longueuil.

Classes are held every week on alternating Fridays and Saturdays from 8 a.m. to 5:30 p.m. All courses are mandatory. A course in small business and entrepreneurship is required, which is unusual for an EMBA. There is a mandatory research paper that students usually start during the summer after first year. It can be a company project, a business plan, or a consulting project. Students also go on a mandatory international trip in the second year of the program. Groups have gone to the Far East and to South America. These trips are open to alumni as well.

In 1996 the program modified its curriculum so that the functional areas are not taught as separate units. "That's not how the issues present themselves in real life. You don't get it in nice little parcels," says Argheyd. In addition there is one integration day per semester where students participate in a simulation or a case competition.

The Bottom Line

What the Judges Think

1998 Concordia International Case Competition: 2nd place

Foreign Affairs

Concordia is a member of CREPUQ, an association of Quebec universities, that gives students access to exchanges with more than 50 universities in the US, Mexico, Australia, England, Denmark, Spain, Italy, the Czech Republic, Sweden, Switzerland, and France. The business school also has two bilateral exchanges with universities in England and Sweden. Despite the plentiful offerings, very few Concordia students go abroad.

Money for Nothing

There is one amazing MBA scholarship worth $20,000 over two years which goes to a female student in the program. There are also two or three much smaller scholarships.

Options

- Master of Science in Administration
- PhD

Contacts

Faculty of Commerce and Administration • Concordia University • 1455 de Maisonneuve Blvd. West • Montreal, QC • H3G 1M8 • (514) 848-2424 • www-commerce.concordia.ca

CONCORDIA UNIVERSITY—VITAL STATISTICS	
total university enrollment	22,255
total full-time undergrad enrollment	10,687
number of full-time professors in the faculty of commerce and administration	121
number of part-time professors	N/A
number of women professors	20 full-time
MBA	
full-time enrollment	126
part-time enrollment	249

size of entering class	60
women students	33%
out-of-province students	2%
international students	2%
students straight from undergrad	none
average age	31
annual tuition for Quebec students	$2,221
annual tuition for Canadian students	$3,421
annual tuition for international students	$9,147
length of program	2 years
number of applications	497
number of acceptances	175
cut-off grade for admission	none
average grade of admittees	3.04 out of 4.3
average GMAT	563
years of work experience required	2
average years of work experience	6
size of core classes	45
size of electives	20 to 30
classes taught by full-time faculty	73%
grads employed within three months of graduation	N/A
number of on-campus recruiters	N/A
grads hired through placement office	N/A
average starting salary	$50,000
what employment figures are based on	33 out of 74 grads of the class of '98

Aviation MBA

enrollment	24

women students	29%
average age	30
international students	96%
average GMAT	508
years of work experience required	3 to 5
average years of work experience	8
cost of program	$34,000
Executive MBA	
enrollment	59
women students	37%
average age	35
average GMAT	517
years of work experience required	5
average years of work experience	12
cost of program	$34,500

Dalhousie University

Dalhousie University in downtown Halifax is very much attached to its image as one of Canada's academic powerhouses. It's a large institution, founded in 1818, with prestigious faculties of law, medicine, and dentistry. Lots of students from outside the Maritimes come here for a change of scene, because it's one of the rare Eastern universities with a name that draws a ripple of recognition elsewhere in the country.

Once upon a time university affairs were simple in Halifax. Catholics went to Saint Mary's; Catholic women went to Mount Saint Vincent; everyone else went to Dalhousie. In the '60s enrollment was high and money flowed like water. But in the early '90s the provincial government turned its attention to the seven post-secondary institutions in the city and began making noises about amalgamating some of them. This bred acrimony—particularly between the business schools at Saint Mary's and at Dal, and each accused the other of wanting to gobble it up. But the threat of amalgamation receded, and both schools have tacitly agreed not to duplicate programs.

It certainly isn't hard for Dal and Saint Mary's to remain distinct. Dal has a small business school in a large university; Saint Mary's has a large business school in a small university. Dal has a Centre for International Business Studies, and in the past tended to rely on a fairly traditional kind of student; Saint Mary's has an Executive MBA, a large part-time MBA, and has aggressively sought to expand this market. Saint Mary's is rah-rah while Dal considers itself more cerebral, or as the Dal saying goes: "Dal is for studying; Saint Mary's is for partying." And there's no doubt that it's harder to get into the business programs at Dal than Saint Mary's.

A-list Alumni

- James Mills MBA '90: President, Office Interiors Inc., The Brewery, Halifax
- Benjamin Gallandar MBA '83: Author of Canadian Small Business Survival Guide, Hounslow Publishing, 1988
- Charles Thomas MBA '75: Retired Commander, Maritime Command
- Harry Mathers MBA '73: Honorary Danish Consul and President, I.H. Mathers & Son Ltd.

In many ways, the government's actions did Dal good, forcing it to think hard about what niche it would occupy. One sign of this is the recent MBA in Financial Services, an innovative program that Dal runs with the Institute of Canadian Bankers (ICB)—the first Canadian MBA program offered in cooperation with a professional organization. Another is the new MBA in Information Technology which Dal began offering in partnership with the Information Technology Institute in 1998, the first time a business school has cooperated with a for-profit educational institution.

Dal has a very attractive campus with lots of elegant ivy-covered buildings. The School of Business Administration is part of the Faculty of Management, along with the schools of public administration, library and information studies, and resource and environmental studies. All are housed in one large building. "It's like a huge old elementary school," says one student fondly. But another complains, "It's just not the glitz that a business building should be." Rumour has it that business was set to get a new building but the law building burned down so the money went there instead.

MBA

Getting In

In 1997-98 the MBA program received 552 applications and accepted 170 of them. Applicants must have a university degree with a minimum grade point average of 3.0 out of 4.0. The average GPA of admitted students was 3.4. Work experience isn't a requirement and about 30% of students come into the program straight from undergrad. Of those who do have the experience, three years is the average. Students with an average grade of 3.3 and an undergrad degree in business can fast-track through the program in 10 months.

Atmospherics

There is excellent spirit in the program. Says one student: "I just love it. I spend every day in the program. You get big groups of people who do everything together." Out of a student body of 200 students, 60 made the trip from Dal to Western to be there for the MBA Games and cheer on their classmates. "The students were really good team workers. It was a great experience because I had been out of school for almost 15 years," one student says. Many are quite involved with the program. A student in the MBA/LLB program, notes: "In law school, I haven't gotten a single e-mail. In the MBA, you get 30 to 40 a week." The program draws students from all over Canada.

Profs, Programs, and Particulars

The two-year MBA has undergone slight revisions, though students still take most of their core courses in first year and most of their electives in second. The core course load has been reduced and material is being integrated across functional areas.

> Dal offers specializations in all the functional areas. The program considers its strengths to be finance, marketing, international business, and information technology. "We don't promote accounting, management science, and HR as much," says Philip Rees, director of the program. As well, there's an array of courses in environmental studies and policy and law, since MBAs have access to the other schools in the faculty of management.

About 30% of MBAs choose Dal for the international business orientation. One of the highlights of the program is the chance to participate in the Foreign Study Mission in Europe. About 30 students apply and 10 are chosen. Students conduct market research in Europe on behalf of Nova Scotia companies. Another international program has students working in Canadian embassies in Trinidad, Malaysia, Brazil, and Washington, as well as in other cities on behalf of Canadian companies.

An externship program is in the pilot stage with six students. They work 12 hours a week in non-paying positions. "It's an opportunity for them to get their feet wet in their field," says Rees.

The overall quality of teaching is good but some complain of inconsistency. "Some profs were very good with the advanced subjects, but were bored by the basic survey courses," a student says. "I wouldn't say it's excellent. I wouldn't say it's terrible. They certainly don't spoon-feed you," another says.

Living It Up

The Dalhousie Association of Graduate Students operates the Grad House on campus. There's also the Grawood Lounge, the Dal pub. Merrill's is the bar of choice in Halifax. Students also go to The Liquor Dome, a big complex with four bars. Other popular pubs are My Father's Moustache, the Thirsty Duck, and J J Rossy's.

There are two student clubs, the MBA Society and the International Business Society. The MBA Society represents MBA students at Dal. They co-ordinate various charitable activities such as Big Brothers and Big Sisters and the Christmas adopt-a-family program.

The faculty has three student-owned small business consulting services: Coburg Consultants Ltd., Maritime Business Consulting, and Atlantic Business Consultants Ltd., the oldest student consulting firm in Canada, founded in 1967. Each year a group of students buys the business from the previous owners. The businesses do production analysis, statistical analysis, and marketing studies.

The Payoff

The school managed to reach 40% of the class of '97 and found that within six months of graduation, 98% of them had found permanent employment. About 45 recruiters come on campus, and 75% of those employed found jobs through career placement. The average starting salary was $52,500.

Gradventures

- Corporate Research Associates Inc., Halifax (Don Mills MBA '74, Greg Trask MBA '75)
- Excel Publishing, Halifax (David S. Towler MBA '80)
- The Graham Group, North York, ON (Gillian Graham MBA '77)
- Marivac Ltd., Halifax (Richard James MBA '75)
- M. April Consultants, Halifax (Michael April MBA '81)

MBA in Financial Services

The MBA in Financial Services is geared toward people who wish to enter the financial services industry or who are already working in it. Students must have completed four ICB courses before applying to the program. The MBA requires completion of 16 courses. Seven are pure ICB courses that are offered intensively over five-day periods in various locations across Canada. These seven courses constitute the Fellow of the ICB designation. The remaining nine are courses from Dalhousie's regular MBA. They cover traditional topics such as accounting, economics, corporate finance, and so forth. Eight of the nine are available only by correspondence except for a three-day intensive session at the end of each course, which is held in a Canadian city where there is sufficient demand. The ninth course, strategic leadership and change, is a capstone course that must be taken at Dalhousie.

MBA in Information Technology

The new MBA in Information Technology is a joint program between Dalhousie and ITI, a Halifax-based for-profit institution which dispenses computer education. Students will have to apply separately to both institutions. Once they are accepted, they will enter ITI full-time while taking a few Dal business courses. After completing the nine-month ITI component, they will spend the remainder of the time at Dal either full-time or part-time. Students who do this MBA full-time will complete the program in 15 months.

The Bottom Line

What the Judges Think

- 1995-96 University of Ottawa High Technology Management Case Competition: 3rd place
- 1995-96 Queen's University Far Horizons Conference: top two papers
- 1994-95 Far Horizons Conference: top two papers

Foreign Affairs

The school of business administration has exchanges with nine universities in Mexico, Denmark, Sweden, South Korea, Germany, France, England, the Netherlands, and Finland. There are two additional exchanges in the works with universities in Australia and New Zealand.

Money for Nothing

MBAs are eligible for 15 scholarships, ranging from $3,000 to $7,000. Fifteen students were employed in the faculty as teaching assistants ($1,200 per year), research assistants ($12 per hour), and graders ($500 per course).

Other Options

- Joint MBA/LLB
- Master of Public Administration

Contacts

School of Business Administration • Dalhousie University • 6152 Coburg Road • Halifax, NS • B3H 1Z5 • (902) 494-7080 • www.mgmt.dal.ca/sba/

DALHOUSIE UNIVERSITY—VITAL STATISTICS

total university enrollment	13,423
total full-time undergrad enrollment	10,885
number of full-time professors in the faculty of management	34
number of part-time professors	6
number of women professors	6 full-time

MBA

full-time enrollment	192
part-time enrollment	43
size of entering class	97
women students	39%
out-of-province students	61%
international students	8%
students straight from undergrad	30%
average age	26
annual tuition	$4,975; $7,570 for the 10-month program
annual tuition for international students	$7,925
length of program	two years; 10 months for business grads
number of applications	552
number of acceptances	170
cut-off grade for admission	3.0 for the two-year program; 3.3 for the 10-month program
average grade of admittees	3.4
average GMAT	594
years of work experience required	none

average years of work experience	3
size of core classes	25 to 45
size of electives	5 to 25
classes taught by full-time faculty	90%
grads employed within six months of graduation	98%
number of on-campus recruiters	45
grads hired through placement office	75%
average base starting salary	$52,500
what employment figures are based on	40% of class of '97

Financial Services MBA

enrollment	162
women students	36%
average age	39
average GMAT	N/A
years of management experience required	5
average years of experience	15
cost of program	$18,500

University of Guelph

Guelph University has long been adept at offering niche programs in business areas at the undergraduate level. The university is one of the few where students can specialize in such subjects as hospitality management, agriculture, and housing and real estate management. So when Guelph's Ontario Agricultural College—John Kenneth Galbraith's alma mater—established an MBA in 1995, it was natural for it to follow the same pattern and offer an MBA in agriculture.

The new MBA program is quite small—in its first year it had about 15 students—but it attracts a high percentage of international students. "The market is not local; it's really much more international than any other MBA program," says Tom Funk, director of the MBA. In January 1997 Guelph also began offering an electronic MBA in agriculture with Athabasca University. Both universities contribute courses to the program. An MBA in hospitality, also delivered through distance education, is in the planning stages.

Established in 1964, Guelph has a pleasing park-like campus with wide lawns and a variety of building styles. Collegiate gothic alternates with concrete, glass, and steel, but the effect is harmonious. There's a nature park to the east of campus, a golf course to the north, cows and more trees to the west, and the city of Guelph to the south, within walking distance.

MBA in Agriculture

Getting In

The typical student in Guelph's MBA in agriculture has an undergraduate degree in some area of agriculture—whether it's horticulture, animal science, soils or veterinary science—and three to five years of relevant work experience. You'll need an average of 70%. Generally, students are not admitted for part-time study except in special cases. In 1997-98 the MBA received 22 applications and accepted 14 of them.

Atmospherics

If your hobby is braiding horses' tails and your dream is to run a rehabilitative farm for abused animals and disabled kids, this is the program for you. A number of people in the program come from farming backgrounds. There are only a handful of students in the program, so relationships tend to be close. The first graduating class is working on putting together an orientation for new students in the program. Because the program is so new, students have had some say in its direction. "We're allowed to provide a lot of feedback about how it could be changed, so we can make it better," says one student.

Profs, Programs, and Particulars

Guelph's MBA in agriculture is a one-year program of four consecutive trimesters. Students must complete 14 core courses that range from standard financial accounting and managerial economics to courses that deal specifically with agriculture, such as agricultural policy. Students must choose three out of seven possible elective courses. In all courses, case studies are taken from the agribusiness industry.

The main contact with industry comes through the individual field consultancy project, in which students have done such things as look at a feed company's distribution system to make it work more efficiently. And the faculty is well connected—Tom Funk, the director of the program, is the grandson of the man who founded the famous feed company Funk Feeds. Students say the program is fairly hands-on. "It makes me feel I can reach out and touch the real world. It's not so academic," says a student.

Living It Up

There aren't any MBA hangouts so far, and students have tended to band together in smaller groups. "We have a blast in the little clique I'm in," says one.

The Payoff

The program has only graduated two batches of students so far. Anecdotally, grads have ended up in a wide variety of jobs, some of them only vaguely related to agriculture.

Electronic MBA in Agriculture

In September 1997 the first cohort of 32 students entered Guelph's MBA in agriculture, offered jointly with Athabasca University. Students spend the first half of the program taking Athabasca courses. They then transfer to Guelph where the remainder of their courses are on-line agriculture courses. Students will likely complete the degree in about three years.

The Bottom Line

Foreign Affairs

There are no exchanges for MBA students.

Other Options

- Master of management studies in hotel and food administration
- Master of science (consumer studies/marketing)

Contacts

Department of Agricultural Economics and Business • University of Guelph • Guelph, ON • N1G 2W1 • (519) 824-4120 ext. 2771 or 3625

UNIVERSITY OF GUELPH—VITAL STATISTICS	
total university enrollment	13,786
total full-time undergrad enrollment	10,454
number of full-time professors	
who teach commerce courses	50
number of part-time professors	N/A
number of women professors	17
MBA in Agriculture	
full-time enrollment	12 to 20
part-time enrollment	none
size of entering class	14
women students	14%
out-of-province students	N/A

international students	N/A
students straight from undergrad	5
average age	27
tuition	$1,575 per semester
tuition for international students	$2,333 per semester
length of program	one year
number of applications	22
number of acceptances	14
cut-off grade for admission	70%
average grade of admittees	75%
average GMAT	not required
years of work experience required	2
average years of work experience	N/A
size of core classes	17
size of electives	N/A
classes taught by full-time faculty	90%
grads employed within six months of graduation	no formal tracking

Electronic MBA in Agriculture

enrollment	60
size of entering class	30
women students	25%
international students	2
students straight from undergrad	none
average age	43
total tuition	$21,500
total tuition for international students	$25,000

length of program	30 months
number of applications	65
number of acceptances	30
cut-off grade for admission	75%
average grade of admittees	75%
average GMAT	not required
years of work experience required	3 to 10
average years of work experience	8
size of core classes	30
size of electives	15
classes taught by full-time faculty	80%

École des Hautes Études Commerciales

Which Canadian business school has the most faculty members? The best—or at least the most expensive—building? The biggest library? The largest number of international exchanges? And more than 9,000 students and 30,000 alumni?

Hint: it isn't York, Western, or the University of British Columbia. Ever heard of the École des Hautes Études Commerciales (HEC)? Other business school deans are always asking Jean-Marie Toulouse, director of this Montreal school, how big the place is and gasping when he tells them. HEC's obscurity in English Canada is principally a result of the fact that it is a francophone institution. In Quebec, HEC is the natural choice for a francophone interested in business. "The French-Canadian bourgeoisie was so small for so long that everyone went to the same school," explains one student.

> For the perfectly bilingual, HEC offers an excellent education with a different flavour. "I wanted to have a different look at the way business is run," says an MBA alum. "I knew that wherever I went, I would hear about the IBMs and the Procter & Gambles, but I thought I might also hear about the Provigos at HEC."

At HEC, you'll still find preppies from Outremont, the leafy French equivalent of Westmount, but you'll also find other Franco-Canadians, Europeans looking for North American business in a familiar language, and citizens from the former French colonies of North Africa. Ironically, HEC is better known outside Canada than in. It bears the same name as a very prestigious Parisian business school, and in countries where French is spoken, HEC is virtually a trademark.

Though HEC-Montreal is modelled on HEC-Paris, it isn't actually related to the French institution. It was founded in 1907 by the Montreal Chamber of Commerce and is now affiliated with the Université de Montréal. It's a well-connected school where professors' contracts require them to devote one day a week to consulting activities. Because its link to the university is looser than that of a traditional business school, it's easier for HEC to enact changes in its programs.

In fact, HEC recently revamped its MBA. The MBA is now one year long, bringing it in line with European competitors such as INSEAD. The program requires students to purchase an IBM ThinkPad upon enrollment, and all courses are geared toward the use of this technology. At the same time, Toulouse vows that HEC's lack of visibility in Canada is coming to an end. All students must now meet certain English language requirements by the time they graduate, and 20% of MBA courses are taught in languages other than French, mostly in English and and a few in Spanish. HEC's alumni are happy about these changes. "English should be a lot more present in the program," says a former student.

A-list Alumni

- Lucienne Robillard MBA '86: Minister of Citizenship and Immigration, Government of Canada
- Martin Thibodeau MBA '85: President, Quebec Metal Powders Ltd.
- Jean Pierre Louise MBA '84: President and CEO, JPL International Inc.
- Pauline Marois MBA '76: Minister of Health, Government of Quebec
- George Rochas MBA '74: Vice-President, Marketing, Air France

In 1996 HEC moved into a luxurious new $100-million building that looks more like a big international agency than a university edifice. "We have a huge set of stairs outside, like the Sorbonne in Paris, so I'm expecting students to sit there and talk to each other. The sun comes out at the end of the day exactly in front of the stairs, so that will be a meeting place, and a business school should be a meeting place," says an administrator. Since fall of 1998, HEC has also had its very own trading room with real-time financial data links—the first in a Canadian business school.

MBA

Getting In

HEC will not say how many applications it received for its new MBA, nor how many of these it accepted. Applicants need a university degree with a minimum average of 70%. The average grade is 75%. HEC requires either the GMAT or the HEC MBA admission test, which tests verbal and analytical ability but is given in French. In any case, the school puts more value on work experience than on the GMAT. Two years of relevant experience are required and most students have closer to eight years. You also have to be able to speak French, since most classes are given in French. Many of the readings, however, are in English and it's possible to write some exams and papers in English. Bilingualism and even trilingualism count in a candidate's favour.

Atmospherics

HEC's MBA attracts a diverse, mature group of students. "I made some great contacts," says a former lawyer who commented that in teams, you might find yourself with an engineer, a doctor, and an economist. There is a large part-time population.

Full-timers who take classes during the day tend to be younger and more focused on their studies, while the part-timers have a lot more experience. "When I was in the part-time program, I thought the students were very interesting. They were less interesting during the day program," says one student.

The student profile is likely to change slightly with the new program. A quarter of the class is already from abroad and the target in five years is to get it up to 50%. Profs are accessible, and each entering student is paired up with a faculty mentor.

Profs, Programs, and Particulars

HEC's new one-year MBA admitted its first class in the fall of 1996. This program spans 54 weeks virtually non-stop, while the old program had 60 weeks of classes spread over two years. Classes have been shortened so that instead of containing 45 course hours, they now contain only 15. Most of the first year of the old MBA has been squeezed into the first two phases of the program. Phases one and two of the program teach business fundamentals and expose students to management issues. The material is integrated and taught cross-functionally. Each of these phases lasts 10 weeks, and students go through them in teams.

Phase three is devoted to specializations. In addition to old standbys like investment and portfolio management, marketing and corporate finance, HEC has added multidisciplinary concentrations in entrepreneurship, management of technological innovation, international management, and management of service companies. One of the strengths of the program is the number and variety of courses, more than 100, that are available to students. This phase lasts 20 weeks.

Phase four, the final 10 weeks of the program, deals exclusively with managing change, everything from Changing Oneself to Managing Strategic Change. Students must participate in a team consulting project, which is supervised by a group of professors. The final grade is given by the professors and by the company.

HEC's MBA used to be known for its focus on the case study method, a fact that drew many former students to the school. While the school still relies on the case study to some degree, it's now just one in an array of teaching methods.

Typically, cases have been taken from Quebec, Canadian, and international companies.

> **Gradventures**
>
> - Air Transat (François Legault MBA '84)
> - Saine Marketing (Jean Saine MBA '80)
> - Strategem (Jacques Dorion MBA '74)

Profs get high marks for experience in industry and for teaching skill. "Out of 22 courses I took, only two professors were disappointing. The rest of them were all great," says an alumna. One alumna mentioned that she chose her courses according to the professors' CVs in the faculty handbook.

Living It Up

HEC's new building is a 15-minute walk from the old building, so chances are that many of the hangouts will remain the same. The Salon Rose is a campus bar with tables and couches. The Côte des Neiges area is home to numerous restaurants, like Crocodile and Kalimera.

There are fewer opportunities for involvement at the MBA level, since many students study part time and have families. The one student club is the Association des Étudiants MBA (AEMBA). It publishes the *Réseau* newsletter, brings in speakers, and runs an annual MBA Career Forum. It also organizes a variety of social activities, such as happy hour for students.

The Payoff

Students are very pleased with the level of service that they receive from the placement office, but some feel glum when they talk to their counterparts at McGill and hear about the companies that post there. About 75% of MBAs use the placement office and of those, 94% find permanent employment within six months of graduation. Top employers include the banks, pharmaceutical companies, finance companies, and caisses de dépôt et placement. The average starting salary is $60,000 with a range between $35,000 and $120,000.

The Bottom Line

Money for Nothing

The MBA program has a total of $50,000 which it awards in scholarships, ranging in value from $500 to $3,000.

Other Options

- Master of science in administration
- PhD

Contacts

École des Hautes Études Commerciales • 3000 chemin de la Côte-Sainte-Catherine • Montréal, QC • H3T 2A7 • (514) 340-6000 • www.hec.ca

ÉCOLE DES HAUTES ÉTUDES COMMERCIALES—VITAL STATISTICS	
total enrollment at HEC	9,200
number of full-time professors	175
number of part-time professors	about 200
number of women professors	43
MBA	
full-time enrollment	120

part-time enrollment	500
size of entering class	120 full-time; 180 part-time
women students	40%
out-of-province students	N/A
international students	25%
students straight from undergrad	none
average age	32
total tuition for Quebec students	$3,026
total tuition for Canadian students	$5,476
total tuition for international students	$15,276
length of program	1 year
number of applications	N/A
number of acceptances	N/A
cut-off grade for admission	70%
average grade of admittees	77%
average GMAT	not required
years of work experience required	2
average years of work experience	6
size of core classes	50
size of electives	30 to 35
classes taught by full-time faculty	75%
grads employed within six months of graduation	94%
number of on-campus recruiters	N/A
grads hired through placement office	N/A
average starting salary	$60,000
what employment figures are based on	85 out of 90 grads from the class of '98

Laurentian University

Laurentian University has the modest ambition of catering to its market. Founded in 1960, this bilingual university serves the francophone and anglophone inhabitants of Sudbury in Northern Ontario. "We are out of the mainstream. We are not in Southern Ontario where there are five or six programs back to back. Very few people take the pain to come to an MBA program in Northern Ontario," says Ozhand Ganjavi, director of the MBA.

> Laurentian offers an MBA that is almost entirely part time. In any given year, about half the students hail from the mining companies in the area. These students have taken a hard look at where they are and have taken the pragmatic route. "Most MBAs are committed to the community because this is where they have set up their lives. It was, 'This is what I've chosen to do and this is where I have to do it,'" says an alumna. The MBA also provides courses to students in Timmins, through videoconferencing.

One thing that incontestably sets Laurentian apart is its reliance on the case-study method. The founders of the School of Commerce and Administration were trained at Western and brought the method with them when they came to Laurentian. New faculty who don't have experience with the method are shipped off to Western to attend case-study seminars. "But we're not fanatic about it," adds Ganjavi. "We determine which teaching technique is more efficient under certain circumstances."

Laurentian has a pretty campus that is more easily imagined in winter than summer. Outdoor activities are big here. It's possible to cross-country ski on campus and there is an outdoor skating rink. The campus is about one kilometre from end to end and has a large lake beside it. The few buildings are large and modern. Business takes up three floors in the Frazier Building.

MBA

Getting In

In 1997-98 the MBA received about 33 applications and accepted 12 of those. Students need a minimum of 70% to be admitted to the program. The average grade of entering students is about 75%. Most students study part time and at least two years of work experience are required for this stream. Recently, the program started accepting full-time students as well but work experience is not a requirement for them. The MBA will accept students who don't have an undergraduate degree provided they have 10 years of work experience. Students may enter the program in April or September.

Atmospherics

Most of the students in the MBA are working professionals. There is a high concentration of people from the mining industry but the program also draws people from government, health care, and law. "There's the stimulation and challenge that comes from people from a variety of backgrounds," one student says.

All courses are offered at night. A few are offered during the day, but even if you're a full-timer, count on taking most of your classes at night. The faculty is good at catering to part-timers, but the administration of the university as a whole could do better, says one student. Marks are sometimes slow to be sent to students and bookstore hours are such that part-timers must take time off work to buy a book.

In a part-time program there isn't the close connection between students, but the program is small enough that students get a lot of personal attention. "I was never an anonymous face, which can happen in some programs," one says.

Profs, Programs, and Particulars

Laurentian's MBA is geared toward general management. "That's what the market demands. If you have limited resources you put it where there is the greatest demand," says Ganjavi. There are 15 required courses and five electives. The majority of electives fall in the areas of human resources management, marketing, and finance—areas that, again, have the most demand.

Almost all instruction is by the case-study method. But because classes are small—never more than 15 people—it's much more of an informal discussion that can be made relevant to the participants. "I really like the method," says one student. "Not only do you learn the concepts, but you start to know about a lot of companies."

Because of the small size of the program, course selection isn't huge. You can cobble together a selection of three courses at most that have the same general topic. "Toward the end when you're taking all electives there could have been more choice," one student says. "The selection is limited," says a student who works as a mining engineer, "but for most people in the mining industry it's definitely enough." There is also the option of taking a research course in an area you're interested in.

Living It Up

When class ends at 10 p.m. most people are thinking about their alarm clocks, not about getting together with other classmates. There is a sense of camaraderie but people don't socialize much. "This is just one part of my life; my life has lots of other parts," one student remarks.

The Payoff

The majority of students are employed when they start the program and remain at the same job afterward.

The Bottom Line

Foreign Affairs

Laurentian has two international exchanges with universities in France and England. The faculty is considering adding a specialization in international business, so the number of exchanges is likely to increase.

Money for Nothing

There are no scholarships for MBA students. Three MBAs work as graduate teaching assistants at a salary of $6,330 a year.

Contacts

School of Commerce • Laurentian University • 955 Ramsey Lake Rd. • Sudbury, ON • P3E 2C6 • (705) 673-6540 • www.laurentian.ca/www/commerce/index.htm

LAURENTIAN UNIVERSITY—VITAL STATISTICS

total university enrollment	5,000
total undergrad enrollment	4,600
number of full-time professors in the faculty of commerce	28
number of part-time professors	7
number of women professors	7 full-time

MBA

full-time enrollment	10
part-time enrollment	70
women students	35%
out-of-province students	none
international students	5%
students straight from undergrad	5%
average age	35
tuition	$419 per half course
annual tuition for international students	$8,400
length of program	2 years
number of applications	33
number of acceptances	12
cut-off grade for admission	70%
average grade of admittees	75%
average GMAT	578
years of work experience required	2
average years of work experience	5 to 7
size of core classes	10 to 15
size of electives	8 to 10
classes taught by full-time faculty	100%
grads employed within six months of graduation	most are already employed

Université Laval

Université Laval's Faculté des sciences de l'administration (FSA) has something no one else has: its own Greek god—Hermes, patron of commerce (and of thieves). The north-east entrance to the school has an impassive statue of him, each academic prize is known as an "Hermès," and you can read about the myth of Hermes on the faculty's Web pages. You would be right to conclude that tradition is important at this university.

For all its prestigious past, the university is little known in English Canada. Its main rival, the École des Hautes Études Commerciales (HEC) in Montreal, is widely considered to be the best French-language business school and one of the top schools in Canada, but even HEC is plagued by lack of visibility. Laval even more so. Part of it is the school's location: Quebec City is just not a centre for big business. Part of it has been the school's insularity. "Laval has realized that it has to be much more in tune," says Robert Mantha, associate dean of the faculty. "It catered basically to the business community in

Quebec, but it's no longer a closed market." Conventional wisdom around the school has it that HEC is great at marketing itself while Laval is not. "The biggest weakness of this faculty is that they don't know how to sell themselves," says a former student who groans when Hermes is mentioned.

But Laval is in transition. There used to be two MBA programs, a specialized MBA similar to an MSc that attracted people coming straight from undergrad and a general MBA designed for people with several years' experience. These two MBAs have been rolled into one completely redesigned program that started in September 1997. MBA LAVAL includes optional internships and interdisciplinary specializations. Best of all, some students will be able to finish the program in as little as 12 months.

> Laval is counting on increased status thanks to its 1995 accreditation by the American Assembly of Collegiate Schools of Business (AACSB). Laval is the only francophone university in the world to have received this honour. In order to receive accreditation, business schools must meet stringent requirements that cover everything from the faculty's mission to the percentage of professors with PhDs (94% at Laval). Getting accredited is hard work, and accreditation can certainly increase a faculty's visibility.

Laval's history stretches back to 1663 when Monseigneur de Laval, the first bishop of New France, founded the Séminaire de Québec. The institution received its university charter in 1852 and promptly became l'Université Laval. The business school, which will be getting a needed facelift, is in the Pavillon Palasis-Prince, a massive Art Deco structure named for the Brother who directed the school from 1924 to 1941.

MBA

Getting In

In 1997-98 the new program received 725 applications and accepted 456. The minimum grade point average for admission is 3.22 out of 4.33 and the average was 3.3. In the new program work experience is preferred but not required; in 1997-98 students had an average of three years' experience.

Atmospherics

The two MBAs attracted different clienteles. The specialized MBA was made up of many students who had just graduated from the BAA. It tended to attract foreign students, particularly for the international business option. For these students, the MBA was a continuation of the high activity level of undergrad. The general MBA catered to an older group of people from the region who had significant work experience. In addition to the old audience, MBA LAVAL is targeting people who are changing jobs and careers.

Profs, Programs, and Particulars

MBA LAVAL started in September 1997. The new program is shorter and students may be able to complete it in as little as a year, depending on their background. It's shorter partly because time is being used more efficiently—no more wind-up and wind-down weeks—and partly because the core is now taught in an integrated fashion, so that there is less redundancy.

> The new program offers specializations in finance, management information systems (MIS), manufacturing management, international business, management, marketing, operations management, accounting, entrepreneurship, and agribusiness management. Strengths include MIS and finance. Operations research is particularly strong, and Laval has the largest such department in Quebec. The operations department was ranked first in Canada for the number of professors receiving grants. Marketing "has had its ups and downs," says Nabil Khoury, former dean of the faculty.

The MBA instituted a new stream in pharmaceuticals, run jointly with the faculty of pharmacy. The stream started in September 1998 and is open to those who have completed a Bachelor of Pharmacy or a science degree. As well, the agribusiness stream now offers a series of courses on-line. There is a proposal with the Université of Montpellier in France to extend this MBA stream to students studying in countries around the Mediterranean.

Students may do a 12-credit project, either applied or research. About 20% of students choose the applied project and spend several months doing an internship.

Gradventures
• Groupe Informission inc. (Jacques Topping MBA '84)
• Les Industries Amisco ltée (Martin Poitras MBA '59)
• Unibroue (André Dion MBA '63)

Living It Up

MBAs go to Le Prolo along with the undergrads. MBAs also have their own lounge in the building. A popular off-campus bar is Le Cactus. There is one club for MBAs, l'APMAL (Association des participants à la maîtrise en administration de Laval). MBAs are less involved in clubs than the undergrads, but "the ones that are involved are really devoted," says a student.

The Payoff

Students go through the same centralized placement office as the undergrads. The most recent study of MBA employment was completed in 1994. It showed that 93% of grads had found employment within 6 months of graduation. According to the placement centre, students without work experience have starting salaries ranging from $28,000 to $42,000. Those with work experience can expect to receive salaries as high as $50,000.

> **A-list Alumni**
>
> - Christian Chagnon MBA '87: First Vice-President, Strategic Planning, Le Groupe Vidéotron ltée
> - Robert Grimard MBA '78: Senior Vice-President and Director, Midland Walwyn Capital
> - Charles Sirois MBA '78: President and CEO, Teleglobe Inc.
> - Gilles Bélanger MBA '71: President, Canadian Trucking Association
> - Jean-Claude Villiard MBA '70: President, SNC-Lavalin Capital Inc.

The Bottom Line

What the Judges Think
1996 MBA Games: 1st place

Foreign Affairs
The FSA has exchanges with 28 universities in Chile, Columbia, Mexico, Peru, the US, Germany, England, Belgium, France, Sweden, and the Czech Republic, and with Simon Fraser, the University of Manitoba, York, and Memorial, in Canada.

Money for Nothing
MBAs are eligible for 27 scholarships worth between $1,000 and $21,500. The most common award is $4,000. In 1995-96, 73 students worked as teaching assistants, nine worked as research assistants, and nine taught undergraduate courses for $16.20 an hour.

Other Options
- Master of Science in Administration
- PhD

Contacts

Faculté des sciences de l'administration • Pavillon Palasis-Prince • Université Laval • Cité Universitaire • Quebec, QC • G1K 7P4 • (418) 656-2180 • www.fsa.ulaval.ca

UNIVERSITÉ LAVAL—VITAL STATISTICS

total university enrollment	33,724
total full-time undergrad enrollment	18,074
number of full-time professors in the FSA	97
number of part-time professors	N/A
number of women professors	21
MBA	
full-time enrollment	312
part-time enrollment	304
size of entering class	260
women students	51%
out-of-province students	2%
international students	27%
students straight from undergrad	40%
average age	30
annual tuition for Quebec students	$2,208
annual tuition for Canadian students	$2,500
annual tuition for international students	$10,128
length of program	16 months
number of applications	725
number of acceptances	456
cut-off grade for admission	3.22 out of 4.33
average grade of admittees	3.3

average GMAT	not required
years of work experience required	none
average years of work experience	3
size of core classes	30
size of electives	25
classes taught by full-time faculty	95%
grads employed within six months of graduation	93%
number of postings	486
grads hired through placement office	N/A
average starting salary	$28,000 to $50,000
what employment figures are based on	N/A

University of Manitoba

The University of Manitoba's Faculty of Management aspires to be a national school. As part of this strategy, the faculty acquired its first dean from the private sector in 1988, William Mackness, a senior vice-president with the Bank of Nova Scotia. But the faculty got more excitement than it had bargained for. The new dean made sweeping changes. He also either offended a reactionary academic culture or, depending on who you talk to, alienated everyone with his abrasiveness. In any case, Mackness was denied reappointment in 1995 and left as the first students were entering MBA MANITOBA, the new program that was almost entirely his creation.

The U of M's MBA was one of the first in Canada to have a shorter 11-month format. It began admitting students with at least three years' managerial experience and in its first year the percentage of domestic students from outside Manitoba jumped from 15% to 30%. It remains to be seen whether these numbers can be sustained, since several other business schools have since moved to shorter programs. (In fact, in 1997-98, the proportion of Manitoba students went back up to 75% from 60%.) Another question is whether the Manitoba market is large enough to support a program with fees of $17,600.

Built in 1987, the new Drake Centre for Management Studies, with its curvy tan exterior, outshines most of the other buildings on campus. These are usually politely described as eclectic. "Our building is like something out of Los Angeles! It's like a movie set! It's the nicest piece of architecture on campus!" gushes one fan. The university's location is less appealing. It's on the outskirts of Winnipeg and commuters can spend more than an hour getting to class.

MBA

Getting In

The MBA program received 100 applications for the full-time class of 1998 and accepted 35 of them. "We actually have a low initial hurdle, but that hurdle is not for admission. That's just for getting to the interview," says Russel Radford, director of the MBA program. You'll need a minimum average of 2.5 out of 4.0 to be admitted to the program (the average grade was 3.25) and three years of managerial work experience. The interview is the critical part of admission. The faculty is looking for people who are enthusiastic, know how to think, and will fit in well with the rest of the class.

A-list Alumni

- Derek Riley MBA '82: President and Partner, NutriLawn International Inc.
- Jacqueline Wolf Scott MBA '81: President, University of Prince Edward Island
- Wayne Walker MBA '76: President, Investors Group Trust Co. Inc., Winnipeg
- Hugh Eliasson MBA '76: Deputy Minister, Department of Government Services, Province of Manitoba
- Stuart Brecken MBA '72: President and CEO, Black Creek Drilling Inc., Houston, Tex.

Atmospherics

The motto of MBA Manitoba could be "everyone does everything." Students go through all classes as a cohort and there are no electives and no exemptions. "If anybody asks if you have a life or if your relationships suffer, it all happens. It's a really strong commitment that's asked of you," says a student. This said, the students are a varied bunch. They may hail from the military, own an ice cream store, or have had diplomatic placements abroad. And they have an average of 11 years' work experience. With so much proximity, people are soon comfortable about speaking up in class.

Profs work closely with the students, who tend to be demanding. "We're a tough audience. We don't let a lot of things slide," says a student. The faculty asks for feedback regularly and has been "100% responsive."

Profs, Programs, and Particulars

In clientele and focus, MBA MANITOBA is similar to an Executive MBA. The program teaches general management with an emphasis on leadership. "You don't have time to develop functional expertise," says Radford. "This is not a school for beginners." Leadership is taught through the professional development days that are scattered throughout the program. (Professors don't "teach" in MBA MANITOBA, they "lead the learning experience.")

Before the program starts, students may attend refresher courses in economics, statistics, and math. The program has three phases: foundations, functions, and strategy and implementation. Phase one is the basics, mainly in lecture format; by phase two, "students have reached the stage where they can effectively integrate and operate as a general staff manager or as a member of a management team," says Radford. Phases two and three have more case work than anything else. Phase three teaches strategy and entrepreneurship and has heavier international content. It culminates in a two-week international trip.

> Most participants cite the practical nature of the program, along with its shorter length, as their principal reason for choosing it. "The majority of our professors have come from the business world, so it's not just theory," says a student. The program beams in international speakers and flies in professors, such as Murray Bryant, former director of the Executive MBA at the University of Toronto, to teach the occasional module.

The main opportunity for field research is the consulting project, usually a meaty project with a Winnipeg company. "Given the nature of the makeup of the class, we have been able to get consulting projects that are substantial," says a student.

All students must participate in the public service project that consists of 40 hours of volunteer work over a six-month period. "We let people see what could be the consequences of decisions they might make as managers," says Radford. Don't think you can get away with stuffing envelopes at the Institute for the Blind.

Gradventures

- Homestead Computers (Sheldon Fulton MBA '72)
- Infocorp Computer Solutions Ltd. (Roy Grant MBA '85)
- Mondetta Clothing (Prashant Modha MBA '91)

Living It Up

"You really have no time for anything—friends, family, social life, volunteer work—and it's hard to balance community service with the consulting project and exams," says a student. People snatch an afternoon between different program phases. Most socializing tends to be informal: faculty barbecues, bingo, pool, bowling, the odd night at Wiseguys or the Faculty Club. The MBA Student Association is the only MBA club.

The Payoff

The Faculty of Management Placement Centre offers the same services to commerce and MBA students, but because of the smaller number of MBAs, they get more one-on-one counselling. The office is geared toward undergrads, however. Three quarters of postings are for jobs that can be filled by commerce or MBA grads, and therefore would probably not suit students with high levels of work experience. About 70 recruiters came looking for MBA students. The placement centre also puts together an MBA résumé book that is distributed through the Associates Network. The dean has written letters of introduction to companies on behalf of students.

The centre surveyed 43 out of 48 grads of the full-time and part-time classes of '98 and found that everyone was employed. Average starting salary was $72,500. Seventeen percent took jobs in the banking/finance/investment area; 17% in the transportation/communications area; 15% in government; 12% in manufacturing; 7% in the health/legal/education area. The remaining 32% were found in a variety of occupations.

The Bottom Line

Foreign Affairs

The faculty of management has 15 exchanges with universities in Brazil, Chile, China, France, Germany, Ireland, Mexico, the Netherlands, South Korea, Turkey, the UK, the US, and one with Université Laval in Quebec.

Money for Nothing

Tuition is high at $17,600, but the program has agreements with four national banks to offer loan packages to students. There are six scholarships for MBA students, ranging in value from $1,000 to $10,000. No students are employed as teaching or research assistants.

Contacts

Faculty of Management • University of Manitoba • Winnipeg, MB • R3T 5V4 • (204) 474-9353 • www.umanitoba.ca/management/index.html

UNIVERSITY OF MANITOBA—VITAL STATISTICS

total university enrollment	21,083
total full-time undergrad enrollment	13,886
number of full-time professors in the faculty of management	53
number of part-time professors	24
number of women professors	9 full-time, 6 part-time
MBA	
full-time enrollment	16
part-time enrollment	125
size of entering class	maximum of 30
women students	30%
out-of-province students	20%
international students	5%
students straight from undergrad	none
average age	35
total tuition	$17,600
total tuition for international students	same
length of program	11 months
number of applications	100
number of acceptances	35
cut-off grade for admission	2.5 out of 4.0

average grade of admittees	3.25
average GMAT	585
years of work experience required	3
average years of work experience	11
size of classes	30
classes taught by full-time faculty	85%
grads employed within six months of graduation	100%
number of on-campus recruiters	70
grads hired through placement office	25%
average starting salary	$72,500
what employment figures are based on	43 out of 48 grads of the class of '98

McGill University

Since the days of Wilder Penfield in the medical school and Hugh McLennan in the English department, people all over the world have kowtowed at the mention of McGill University, and students have flocked there for the name—sometimes only for the name. "The name is golden," says an administrator somewhat smugly. Go to McGill and you can feel good about attending a university people will have heard of outside of Canada.

Thanks to its reputation, McGill attracts a record 51% of international students to its MBA. Often McGill is the only Canadian university these international students have applied to. In addition, many professors in the Faculty of Management are from other countries. And in 1997 McGill began offering an MBA program in Japan.

Management is a research faculty with several big name faculty members. The amazing Henry Mintzberg teaches here, but don't expect to get anywhere near him if you're just an MBA student. (He teaches in the PhD and executive programs and disapproves of MBAs that take in students with minimal work experience.) But many of the other star researchers do teach undergrads and MBAs. The Faculty of Management has several research centres, among them the Centre for the Study of Strategy in Organizations and GÉRAD (Groupe d'études et de recherches en analyse des décisions).

The downside of all this brain power? Rewards accrue to professors for their research rather than for their mentoring, especially at the undergraduate level. Says an administrator: "In terms of being a warm and fuzzy place, we're not. We don't associate that much with each other, let alone with students." Students describe the administration as a lumbering bureaucracy that is more likely to meet student initiatives with, "it's been tried before and it didn't work" than with enthusiasm. "It's hard to throw a new idea at McGill," acknowledges an alumna.

Despite these ills, thousands of students have a wonderful time at McGill. The MBA attracts a high-quality group of people. Extracurricular life is exuberant; so is Montreal, when it's not agonizing over a constitutional crisis. Students appear to consider their experience in the programs to be superior to the programs themselves.

A-list Alumni

- Claire Lanctôt MBA '88: Executive Director, Finance, Bell Canada International (Montreal)
- Alexander Töeldte MBA '85: Principal, McKinsey and Co., Montreal
- Jacqueline Beaurivage MBA '81: Vice-President, Customer Segments, Canadian Imperial Bank of Commerce
- Lili de Grandpré MBA '81: Vice-President, Mercer Management Consulting, Montreal
- Claudio Bussandri MBA '76: President and CEO, Medis Health and Pharmaceutical Services; former President and CEO, Lantic Sugar

McGill is in downtown Montreal. The 1821 campus is classically urban with a green, lots of old crumbly buildings and stately gates. But if you're in management, you don't get to go through the gates. The faculty is in the Bronfman Building, a cramped edifice outside the gates. Griping about the facilities and the miserable funding is a favourite student pastime. (The building isn't even connected to the underground passages that link almost everything else, laments one student.)

MBA

Getting In

In 1997-98 the MBA received 858 applications and accepted 401 of them. On paper you need a 3.0 average, a year's work experience, and a minimum GMAT score of 580. "If we found someone with exactly this profile, we probably wouldn't admit them. We're looking for something exciting about that person," says an administrator. There is some leeway with these requirements. A few students without work experience are admitted to the program. One alumnus who had been denied admission because of grades in the mid 70s remembers going to the admissions office and talking them into accepting him. Students who have an undergraduate degree in business and at least three years work experience are admitted to a 15-month version of the program.

Atmospherics

Ask MBAs the best thing about the program and many will talk about the other students. "It's been an excellent experience for the sheer diversity of people in my class. It brings a certain richness; there's something to learn from everyone," says a second-year MBA student from Nigeria. "We're the only people we hang out with. A lot of us are away from home, and we all get along very well," adds a student from South Africa.

Part-time students, however, are the exception to this happy throng. Many complain of alienation and lack of responsiveness from a school geared to full-time students. "The administration treats us a bit like second-class citizens. They're very slow to respond to our needs," says one part-timer. Students say that the dean's office is responsive to their concerns.

No one is admitted without work experience, yet students speak of large numbers of inexperienced students. As one student says disapprovingly: "Too many students running around with 750 GMAT scores and little experience."

Profs, Programs, and Particulars

The MBA is going into the fourth year of a revised program. All of first year is devoted to the core. Students work in teams throughout. An integrative course concludes each part of the three sections of the core. It's a great idea, say students, but there have been glitches. One problem, now remedied, is that each part of the core was administered by a separate person. Another problem has been assigned groups: for the sake of diversity, one part-timer was put in every group of full-timers, which led to scheduling problems for the part-timers. (According to one student, the group problems had more to do with the students than with the core itself.)

Second year is devoted to specializations. The MBA offers specializations in finance, marketing, entrepreneurial studies, international business, management for development, strategic management, and general management.

> The general management option is geared toward students with substantial work experience. About 40% of students choose this stream. Management for development is a unique specialization spearheaded by some MBA students about three years ago. It's an option for students interested in working in developing countries. Students praise the strategy area.

The program tries to bring an international perspective throughout. But this perspective is provided more by the students themselves. Most companies that are being looked at are still North American. McGill's excellent and abundant foreign exchanges add a lot to the international dimension. Says one student who spent a semester at the Thammasat University in Bangkok: "It was the best experience of my MBA and of my life."

Quality of teaching varies. "In some professors there is a lack of being current with fairly recent business happenings and communications," complains one student. "The best ones we had were the ones doing consulting and teaching in the executive education program," adds another.

The core tends to be fairly academic, but you can make your program more applied in second year. Students can enroll in independent study courses where they might do field research. "In every course, we always had the option to go outside and actually go out into the business community," says an alumnus.

Living It Up

Thomson House is a historic mansion that was turned into a centre for all McGill graduate students. Thursday night is MBA night at Thomson House. Off campus, students gravitate toward St. Laurent Street. Angels and Desalvio's are two popular places.

The McGill MBA Student Council is the umbrella club for many student activities. It runs orientation week and coordinates international potluck dinners that are held every semester, ski trips, and various inter-university case competitions. There are two student consulting groups: the McGill Business Consulting Group (MBCG) and the McGill International Consulting Group (MICG). More than 70 students apply to join the MBCG but only six are chosen ("the toughest interview I've ever done," says one of the lucky six). Both provide consulting to local companies, but the MICG also helps these companies find trading partners abroad. MICG has been involved with projects in Mexico, Pakistan, Thailand, Poland, China, and India.

> **Gradventures**
>
> - First Marathon Securities (Lawrence S. Bloomberg MBA '65)
> - Franco-Nevada Mining Corp. Ltd. and Euro-Nevada Mining Corp. Ltd. (Seymour Schulich MBA '65)
> - Metrix Interlink, internet provider (Robert Quance MBA '84)
> - Repap Enterprises (George Petty B.Comm '54 and MBA '58)
> - Socanav Inc. (Michel Gaucher MBA '69)

The McGill Graduate Business Conference is an annual event organized by MBA students that draws about 170 people. The theme of the conference usually revolves around the area of strategic management. McGill has a chapter of Students for Responsible Business, the first chapter started at a Canadian university. The MBA Gunners are the intramural sports teams that compete in hockey, basketball, and soccer.

The Payoff

The Management Career Centre is an office within the faculty that takes care of both MBA and commerce placement. The centre runs several workshops throughout the year. One-on-one counselling and practice interview sessions are available to all students. Whenever students get another interview, they are automatically scheduled in for an appointment with a counsellor.

In the past students have felt that the office could do more to help them. Part of the problem is circumstantial. "McGill is an English school in a predominantly French province so there's an instant problem," says one foreign student. And there isn't much in the way of positions for international students. "They write us off because we're not going to work here, but companies recruit for offices overseas," says another. According to the Career Centre, many companies are loath to hire international students.

The MCC managed to survey 72% of the class of '98 and found that within a month of graduation, 86% of them were employed full-time. More than half the class found employment through the MCC. One-hundred-and-sixty-five companies came on campus to recruit both MBA and commerce students. Top areas were finance, including financial services; I-banking and commercial banking with 39%; marketing 23%; consulting 18%; and information technology 8%. The average starting salary was $70,000.

The Bottom Line

What the Judges Think

- 1996 Compugen Systems—Toronto MBA "One Day to Run the World!" Business Challenge: 1st place
- 1996 National MBA Games: 1st place, Unilever Business Games Award

Foreign Affairs

The faculty has a network of 20 MBA exchanges with universities in the Philippines, Turkey, Denmark, Holland, Spain, Brazil, Mexico, Pakistan, Italy, England, Norway, Belgium, Sweden, Thailand, Germany, and the US.

Money for Nothing

MBA students from Canada are eligible for six to eight entrance scholarships worth between $1,000 and $1,500; MBAs from abroad are eligible for more than 30 entrance scholarships, ranging from $1,500 to $3,000. There are five other outside scholarships worth between $1,500 and $4,000. An amazing scholarship worth $27,000 goes to an MBA student from Poland; a $5,000 scholarship is awarded to a student from Hong Kong. About 30 MBAs work as research assistants or tutors. Pay is anywhere from $10 to $17.84 an hour.

Other Options

- International Master in Management
- Joint MBA/MD
- Joint MBA/LLB
- Joint MBA/Master of Science in Agricultural Economics
- Master of Management in Manufacturing
- Master of Management in Economic Policy
- PhD

Contacts

Faculty of Management • McGill University • 1001 Sherbrooke St. W. • Montreal, QC• H3A 1G5 • (514) 398-4000 • www.management.mcgill.ca

MCGILL UNIVERSITY—VITAL STATISTICS

total university enrollment	28,473
total full-time undergrad enrollment	14,919
number of full-time professors in the faculty of management	66
number of part-time professors	51
number of women professors	15 full-time
MBA	
full-time enrollment	302
part-time enrollment	268
size of entering class	204
women students	28%
out-of-province students	35%
international students	51%

students straight from undergrad	none
average age	26
annual tuition for Quebec students	$1,668
annual tuition for Canadian students	$2,868
annual tuition for international students	$16,000
length of program	2 years
number of applications	858
number of acceptances	401
cut-off grade for admission	3.0 out of 4.0
average grade of admittees	3.3
average GMAT	615
years of work experience required	1
average years of work experience	3.4
size of core classes	50
size of electives	25 to 45
classes taught by full-time faculty	81%
grads employed within one month of graduation	86%
number of on-campus recruiters	165
grads hired through placement office	77%
average starting salary	$70,000
what employment figures are based on	102 out of 140 grads of the class of '98

McMaster University

David Conrath, dean of the business school at McMaster University, does not want to see a repetition of the following incident. While touring Dofasco Steel Inc. with its CEO, he began chatting about the MBA co-op program. The CEO answered, "I didn't know McMaster had a co-op program," unaware that several employees in the room were Mac grads whose co-op placements had been at Dofasco.

These days the Michael G. DeGroote School of Business in Hamilton, Ontario, is working hard to mitigate its beigeness. It positions itself now as the business school with the most to offer in terms of real-world experience. The MBA continues to accept students without work experience, but it is now impossible to graduate without it, thanks to the excellent co-op program—the largest in Canada despite its lack of visibility. Only those with previous work experience are exempted from co-op.

> The most recent addition to the school is a trading-room with real-time financial data links, one of two at a Canadian university (the other is at the École des Hautes Études Commerciales). The room became operational in January 1999 and is housed in a new building adjacent to the business school. CIBC Wood Gundy, whose chair is a Mac MBA grad, is providing the data and has given money for a new chair to be involved with the trading room.

But McMaster can't seem to resign itself to how it thinks others see its home town. "People just don't believe something this good is happening in Hamilton. They say it's a steel town, a lunch-box town. But London or Kingston, they say it's a booky kind of intellectual community," says professor Marvin Ryder. When the slogan "Learning to work—Working to learn" was coined to promote the changes in the programs, some professors complained that it sounded too working class. (To its credit, Mac kept the slogan.)

The university is in Westdale, a quaint residential part of Hamilton that borders on a conservation area. Mac has a very pretty campus that even looks good on grey-brown winter days and is lovely in the spring and fall. The business school is in a smart new building that was built entirely with private money. Even the bookcases in the Innis business library have their own individual donors.

MBA

Getting In

The MBA program received 582 applications for entry in 1998 and accepted 250. The cut-off is a B, and the average grade hovers between B+ and A-. Work experience isn't required or even preferred but about 45% have an average of three years' experience. Mac does accept qualified applicants who don't have an undergraduate degree.

Atmospherics

The MBA students used to have a pride problem. "There was disgruntlement about how they perceived that they were perceived," explains one alum. But a few years ago, the MBA executive created the Pride program, meant to cheer MBAs up about their education and their school. It seems to have worked. "We want to communicate to everyone what a fine program exists here. I am certainly proud to be a McMaster student," says the former president of the MBA association. Many students (and grads) are pleased with the efforts of the dean to promote the school and say his office is receptive to their concerns.

As a group, the MBA students are fairly young (at 26, about three years younger than the national average) and slightly more than half come straight from undergrad. The program attracts very few international students. The Outward Bound orientation, run by second-year MBAs for the incoming class, helps bring everyone together. Everyone goes to Lake Couchiching for team-building and leadership exercises: climbing 12-foot walls with your teammates and the like.

Profs, Programs, and Particulars

The MBA program has a new core. The program starts with workshops on team skills and critical thinking. Students then take 20 first-year courses that are all six-weeks long. This allows students to get more exposure to all of the business disciplines earlier on. "Going into a first work term, it's really helpful to have the six-week courses, even just for the terminology," says an MBA student. But the short courses take some getting used to. "The biggest problem was professors who hadn't adapted to the format," says another student.

> Specializations are one of Mac's strong suits. In second year, students choose one of 10 streams. In addition to standard areas such as general business, international business, accounting, information systems, management science/operations management, finance, human resources/labour relations, and marketing, there are interdisciplinary streams such as health services management and management of innovation and new technology (MINT), in which students take advanced courses in a technical field such as computer science or engineering. "We're trying to get away from discipline-based streams," says Trevor Chamberlain, the associate dean. Finance is particularly strong, as is management science, though few students are interested in the latter. New finance courses in commodities and foreign exchange will take advantage of Mac's new trading room. McMaster recently added a specialization in electronic commerce to its offerings.

Students say that the program still has a heavy quantitative orientation. "For someone going into marketing and HR, there's probably more number crunching than they need. But having as solid a numbers background as possible can only help," says one student. One former finance major remembers, "A lot of us were silently screaming for more applicability." But co-op brings in the real-world experience. "Every time you'd go to the workplace you'd say, 'Oh, this is what you mean,'" says a co-op grad.

Gradventures

- Bob Clute Pontiac Buick GMC Ltd. (Bob Clute MBA '76)
- Dominion Bond Rating System (Walter Schroeder MBA '69)
- Fitness Depot (Mark Dubois MBA '80)
- Langley Parisian Ltd. (Ken Adamson MBA '76)
- Save-Smart (Steve Sardo MBA '82)

Co-op

Co-op is one of the major strengths of this MBA. Admission is by interview and the criteria are grades, attitude, focus (you need to have some idea of your interests), and, to some degree, previous job experience. The placement rate is 100%. There is a minimum of three four-month work terms.

Between 45% and 60% of employers are in the Greater Toronto Area. The Ottawa high-tech industry usually accounts for another 10% to 20%. About 10% are international, usually jobs that students have found on their own. And there are some positions in London, Calgary, and Vancouver. Average monthly salary for a first work term is $2,528; for a second work term, $2,632; and for a third, $2,787. Salaries in the health services management option tend to be a little lower than the general business ones. The vast majority of employers are in the private sector. Even in health management, opportunities in the private sector are increasing. Traditionally jobs have been clustered in telecommunications, banking, and high-tech. Growing areas are manufacturing and consulting.

> **Most popular co-ops:** it varies. In the past couple of years finance jobs have been hot. In the most recently admitted class, marketing and human resources jobs are especially popular.
>
> **Least popular co-ops:** government—both by choice and by necessity. In the general stream, government is seen as "big and blue. You don't necessarily want to be there," says a co-op alum. Some health management students would like to work in the public sector but feel that it holds no promise for a permanent job.

Living It Up

The Phoenix, Mac's grad pub, is the main hangout for MBA students. Lunch places are the Togo Salmon Cafeteria and the Wokery, another McMaster cafeteria. The Snooty Fox, The

Border, and Monopoly are three off-campus bars that are frequented on a semi-regular basis. The Bean Bar is a popular coffee and cake place across from The Snooty Fox. For small restaurants and cafés, people head to Hess Street, a beautiful old cobblestone street in downtown Hamilton.

The main MBA club is the MBA Association. It runs the National Business Conference with the Commerce Society. The conference brings in nationally and internationally renowned senior executives. It's a big deal on campus, says an undergrad: "Our one gold coin." He's quickly corrected by a classmate: "One of our gold coins."

The Payoff

Business Career Services keeps track of every single one of its co-op grads and says that all are employed within six months of graduation. BCS surveyed 72% of the full-time non-co-op grads and found that 93% were employed within the same time frame. In 1997-98, 260 organizations recruited MBAs. Many students end up in finance, production, or marketing. The overall average starting salary was $56,615. Students with no work experience except co-op netted average starting salaries of $51,030; average salary of those with previous work experience was $62,200. Salaries ranged from a high of $114,000 (excluding bonus) to a low of $40,000.

The career office runs customized workshops for MBA students. The office also alerts students to interesting opportunities by e-mail. Students could not say enough about the co-op service, but some felt that permanent placement was not quite as good.

A-list Alumni

- Arthur Church MBA '84: President and CEO, Champion Road Machinery Ltd.
- Jonathan Wellum MBA '84: Manager, AIC Advantage Fund (winner of the 1996 Mutual Fund Manager of the Year Award)
- Louise Laccin MBA '83: Vice-President and Treasurer, Loblaw Companies Ltd.
- Shelley Forrester MBA '82: Vice-President and Director, Wood Gundy Inc.
- Claude Brochu MBA '70: President and CEO, Montreal Expos Club

The Bottom Line

Foreign Affairs

The business school has exchanges with seven universities in France, Norway, Mexico, Germany, the UK, and Singapore.

Money for Nothing

There are 25 MBA scholarships worth between $500 and $10,000. Sixty students are employed as teaching or research assistants for a wage of $2,851 per term, including benefits.

Other Options

PhD

Contacts

Michael G. Degroote School of Business • McMaster University • 1280 Main St. W. • Hamilton, ON • L8S 4M4 • (905) 525-9140 ext. 24431 • www.business.mcmaster.ca

MCMASTER UNIVERSITY—VITAL STATISTICS

total university enrollment	17,013
total full-time undergrad enrollment	12,318
number of full-time professors in the school of business	52
number of part-time professors	9
number of women professors	10

MBA

full-time enrollment	239
part-time enrollment	225
size of entering class	191
women students	37%
out-of-province students	N/A
international students	1%
students straight from undergrad	55%
average age	26 full-time; 30 part-time
annual tuition	$3,968
annual tuition for international students	$12,000
length of program	2 years
number of applications	582
number of acceptances	250
cut-off grade for admission	B
average grade of admittees	B+ to A-
average GMAT	632
years of work experience required	none
average years of work experience	3

size of core classes	30 to 45
size of electives	15 to 35
classes taught by full-time faculty	85%
grads employed within six months of graduation	100% co-op; 93% non-co-op
number of on-campus recruiters	260
grads hired through placement office	N/A
average starting salary	$51,030 for those without work experience $62,200 for those with experience
what employment figures are based on	44 out of 51 grads of '98 co-op class

Memorial University

It's a safe bet that if Memorial University of Newfoundland (MUN) weren't actually in Newfoundland, its Faculty of Business Administration with its good quality MBA program would have a much higher profile. As a student says: "There's a certain stigma surrounding the province—that it's floundering in economic dismay."

As the only university in Newfoundland, MUN, which was founded in 1925, has a mission to minister to the province. After graduation, most MBA students stay in St. John's, where they are found throughout the business community. One of the faculty's research arms, the P. J. Gardiner Institute for Small Business, runs the New Enterprise Stores to help would-be entrepreneurs start their own businesses. In 1995 the program had a 70% success rate. "We get the university a lot of good press, which helps in its negotiations with the government," says Bill Blake, dean of the faculty. Outside of Newfoundland, the business school has been gaining a national profile through its phenomenal showing in events such as the the MBA International Case Competition at Concordia.

MUN's campus is split in two by the crosstown arterial. The professional schools are on one side, everything else is on the other. "It's almost like two different universities," says a student. Skywalks connect the two halves of campus. Buildings are a hodge-podge of styles. The school of business is one of the newest buildings on campus with an atrium in its centre and lots of glass and skylights. Thanks to a recent $150,000 donation from Mobil Corp., the faculty has built several new super-classrooms.

MBA

Getting In

The MBA program received 100 applications in 1997-98 and sent out 65 acceptances. Most students are part-timers, though the number of full-timers has been steadily increasing. Students need a minimum average of B to be considered for the program. There's no work experience requirement, but because of all the part-timers, the average number of years of experience is high, at seven. Under special circumstances, the faculty may accept some students without an undergraduate degree. Students who come in with a previous degree in business can now complete the MBA in one year.

Atmospherics

Despite its part-time character, the program is noted for its close ties. One MBA student with three previous degrees from MUN, noted that she had not encountered the same level of closeness in other graduate departments in the university. "It's really co-operative," says another. "I had computer problems at the beginning and two to three people spent several hours helping me."

Profs, Programs, and Particulars

Memorial's MBA is a general management program. It is being revamped bit by bit and any further changes are likely to happen incrementally. New courses have been added in management of change, project management, international business, innovation, and technology in the Canadian environment. In addition, management of technology, entrepreneurship, and change innovation have become required courses. One elective must now be taken in the international area.

The curriculum is also moving slowly toward integration and team teaching. A management skills course, including leadership and negotiation skills, taught by three faculty members, was recently added to the curriculum. You can't get through the program without learning how to do a decent presentation. There is a strong emphasis on teamwork. Enthusiasm for this depends on how much time you have. "I have a very busy life. Group work takes a lot of time," says a former student flatly, while another student declares, "I've learned so much about working with groups."

> The high level of work experience is a boon both to other students and to professors. "It's one thing to instruct a group who is just happy to get through the program and get the piece of paper. But because they deal with a majority of mature students who can relate to a work environment or human resources, the profs take the program more seriously," says a student who is a third of the way through the program.

While students excel at case competitions, there is no one method of instruction. Lectures, cases, readings, and discussions are all routine. "We run the whole gamut in terms of how we teach; I think that's wise," says Herb MacKenzie, director of the MBA. The program strikes a good balance between theory and practice.

There are several opportunities for field research. Independent research projects are one possibility. Students have done such projects as helping a municipality with its information system. Students can also work in the P. J. Gardiner Institute advising local small businesses.

The faculty has begun offering a one-year modularized version of the MBA to a group of Chinese managers who work for foreign multinationals in St. Johns.

Gradventures

- Atlantic Group of Companies (Kevin Brew MBA '90)
- Insight Inc. (Ann Rose MBA '93)
- Cable Bahamas (Rick Pardy MBA '81)

Living It Up

Most socializing between classmates takes place on campus. There are always lots of people in the MBA lounge between classes. Other on-campus hangouts include: the Thomson Student Centre; the grad bar, Bitters; and the Breezeway, the student-owned campus bar, which is one of the most profitable campus bars in Canada.

The Payoff

The majority of students are already employed when they start the program and remain in their jobs afterward.

> **A-list Alumni**
>
> - Joseph D. Randell MBA '85: President and CEO, Air Nova Inc.
> - John Abbott MBA '85: Managing Director, Investment Banking Services, Alberta, Nesbitt Burns Inc.
> - Darlene Kruesel Hyde MBA '82: Vice-President, Public Affairs and Road Safety, Insurance Corp. of British Columbia

The Bottom Line

What the Judges Think

MBA International Case Competition at Concordia: 1st place (1996), 2nd place (1995), 3rd place (1993)

Foreign Affairs

Memorial has a Centre for International Business Studies with a mandate that includes promoting international exchanges. There are 12 formal exchange programs in different European countries, including one at Memorial's campus in Harlow, north of London, UK. A small number of MBAs go on exchange every year.

Money for Nothing

MBA scholarships are available to full-time students only. There are seven of them, five at $1,000, one at $3,000 and another at $5,000. Five or six students per term work as assistants, doing library searches, invigilating exams, running computer simulations, and in some cases doing research. The pay is $750 for 56 hours of work.

Contacts

Faculty of Business Administration • Memorial University • St. John's, NF • A1B 3X5 • (709) 737-8854 • www.mun.ca/business

MEMORIAL UNIVERSITY—VITAL STATISTICS

total university enrollment	15,822
total full-time undergrad enrollment	11,913
number of full-time professors in the faculty of business administration	40
number of part-time professors	42
number of women professors	9

MBA

full-time enrollment	65
part-time enrollment	141
size of entering class	50
women students	44%
out-of-province students	6%
international students	5%
students straight from undergrad	8%
average age	32
annual tuition plus fees	$6,000
annual tuition plus fees for international students	same
length of program	2 years
number of applications	100
number of acceptances	65
cut-off grade for admission	B
average grade of admittees	N/A
average GMAT	580
years of work experience required	none
average years of work experience	7 years

size of core classes	20 to 40
size of electives	10 to 30
classes taught by full-time faculty	95%
grads employed within six months of graduation	most students are already employed

Université de Moncton

"People come to Moncton because they want to continue their education in French," says an MBA student—which often means that if they're Canadian and are in the MBA program, they've already done their undergrad at Moncton. That's because l'Université de Moncton's main *raison d'être* is serving the francophone population of New Brunswick, and its Faculté d'administration is the only French business school outside of the province of Quebec. The university was founded in 1963 to serve the three main French regions of New Brunswick: Shippagan, Edmundston, and Moncton. (The main campus is in Moncton, but there are satellite campuses in the two other cities as well.) Because of this the faculty also attracts lots of international students from the former French colonies of Africa.

The business school overhauled its programs in 1996 and a co-op program was instituted in the regular MBA program in 1997. That same year the faculty started offering what George Wybouw, dean of the faculty, calls "the first multimedia MBA in French in the world." (Computer literacy and the use of technology is a point of pride in the faculty. "E-mail is compulsory," says Wybouw.) The program is a part-time version of the regular MBA that is given through videoconferencing and Internet courses in seven sites in Atlantic Canada and in Toronto and Sudbury. There is talk of adding a site in Gaspésie.

Much of the population of the province is bilingual. All instruction at the university is in French, but many of the readings, especially in the MBA, are in English. The only students who have trouble with English tend to be foreign students or the occasional Quebecer.

The university is in a residential part of the city. It's a pleasant campus on a large hill. Most of the buildings are modern and there's lots of green space.

MBA

Getting In

In 1997-98 the MBA received 100 applications and accepted 60 of those. Applicants need a minimum average of 3.0 out of 4.3 to be considered for admission. The average grade of admitted students is 3.3. Work experience isn't a requirement and increasingly students come in without it. People who have an undergrad degree in business can go directly into second year provided their marks are high enough.

Atmospherics

The program is small, with about 30 new people entering each year. Most of the MBAs tend to be fairly young, especially since the new co-op program attracts people without work experience. Half the MBA student body is from abroad, mainly from North Africa. There are 14 nationalities in the student group.

One does not get the same enthusiasm from the MBAs as from the undergrads. People are pleased enough to be here and hope that the program will open doors for them, but it doesn't go much further. One student complains about callow classmates coming straight from undergrad. "Sometimes I wonder what they're doing in the business field."

Profs, Programs, and Particulars

The MBA is a two-year program that teaches general management. Until the co-op program was started, this orientation led to some lack of direction. "If the co-op program didn't exist, I wouldn't be able to identity what the program's mission is," says a second-year student. "If they had a clearer purpose, it would give a fuller environment for the students."

Students say the program provides good practical experience. In the new program, there is a greater emphasis on projects and working outside the walls of the university. New courses are being introduced in entrepreneurship and small business. Most professors have experience in industry.

> **Co-op**
>
> Since 1997 all students in the regular MBA have been in the co-op program. There are two work terms of 15 weeks each. Students have worked at the Atlantic Canada Opportunities Agency (ACOA), NB Tel, and in a boxing plant that is a subsidiary of Cott Inc.

The program has lots of group work. Groups are chosen by the program director to ensure that they are heterogeneous; they include both men and women, as well as one or two international students, and a variety of academic backgrounds. Because the student body is small, everyone ends up giving at least two presentations per course.

The quality of teaching is reasonably good, "3.5 out of 5," volunteers one student. "I can't say great, but it's been good," says another. There are some theoretical people, some practical people, and then we have the others."

Living It Up

Students hang out in the MBA lounge and at the campus bar, l'Osmose. Off-campus hot spots are the same as for undergrads: Fat Tuesdays and Ziggy's. The MBA student council is the only club, but under it there are various committees. The social committee organizes visits to companies, attendance at conferences, team sports, and parties.

The Payoff

The MBAs use the same service in the student centre as the undergrads and have access to the same recruiters. About 95% of grads are employed within six months of graduation at an average salary of $36,000. Starting salaries range from $28,000 to $60,000.

The Bottom Line

Gradventures

Atlantic Mini Fridge (Dollard Landry MBA '64)

Foreign Affairs

The faculty has exchanges with three universities in France, Guatemala, and Mexico and is in the process of establishing more.

Money for Nothing

There are 15 scholarships for MBA students, ranging from $1,000 to $5,000. The average award is $3,000. About 10 students work as teaching/research assistants for $7 to $8 an hour.

Other Options

Joint MBA/LLB

Contacts

Faculté d'administration • Université de Moncton • Moncton, NB • E1A 3E9 • (506) 858-4446 • www.umoncton.ca/administration

UNIVERSITÉ DE MONCTON—VITAL STATISTICS

total university enrollment	6,013 on all three campuses
total full-time enrollment at Moncton	3,636
total part-time enrollment at Moncton	683
number of full-time professors in the faculty of administration	28
number of part-time professors	15
number of women professors	6 full-time

MBA

full-time enrollment	55
part-time enrollment	120 (multimedia MBA + part-time MBA)
size of entering class	30
women students	45%
out-of-province students	10%
international students	50%
students straight from undergrad	40%
average age	33
tuition	$330 per course
tuition for international students	$480 per course
length of program	2 years
number of applications	100
number of acceptances	60
cut-off grade for admission	3.0 out of 4.3
average grade of admitted students	3.3
average GMAT	not required
years of work experience required	none
average years of work experience	4

size of core classes	30
size of electives	15
classes taught by full-time faculty	90%
grads employed within six months of graduation	95%
number of on-campus recruiters	30
grads hired through placement	50%
average starting salary	$36,000
what employment figures are based on	25 out of 60 grads of the class of '98

University of New Brunswick—Fredericton

The University of New Brunswick's two campuses are like yin and yang. The Saint John satellite campus has a modern 1965 campus, tepid school spirit, and a business school that has branched out into the new area of electronic commerce. The main campus in Fredericton has a postcard-perfect campus that dates from 1785, lots of school spirit, and a business school that attracts a fairly traditional type of student.

> The best thing about Fredericton's MBA is the academic partnering internship, which matches a student up with a company interested in doing business internationally. Students meet with the vice-presidents of the company, do research for them, and then go abroad with them. Past destinations include Mexico, Poland, and Trinidad. "It was a wonderful experience," says one alum who went to Monterrey, Mexico, with a client company. "I didn't have any exposure to international business. You learn how to conduct a meeting with people from a different culture."

Fredericton's campus is as gorgeous as a New England Ivy League school. The university is on a large hill and there are grassy fields in front of the Student Union Building. The oldest university building still in use in Canada is at Fredericton. Most of the buildings are in Georgian red brick, and even the new ones have kept to the same colour scheme.

MBA

Getting In

In 1997-98 the MBA received 200 applications of which it accepted 40. The minimum requirement is an average of 3.0 out of 4.0; the average grade is 3.3. Work experience is not an absolute requirement, though the admissions team prefers students to have at least three years' experience. Among students who do have the experience, the average is about five years. About 10% come in with no work experience at all.

Atmospherics

The MBA program has equal numbers of part-time and full-time students. But with only 30 students starting the full-time program each year, the atmosphere is close-knit and co-operative. "I didn't want to go somewhere like the University of Toronto and get lost in a big university," says a student. There is a lot of group work so students get to know each other quickly. About 10% of the class comes from abroad.

Profs, Programs, and Particulars

Fredericton's MBA has been offered since 1986. Since 1996, all of first year has been taught in an integrated fashion. Courses are taught in six-week modules and a theme-based integrative course, such as management of technology, pulls the material together. "All important business problems are not solely marketing problems or accounting problems," says Norm Betts, associate dean and director of the MBA.

Second year is devoted to electives. The main concentration is in international business but the program has recently put together a package of elective courses in environmental management. There's also an informal linkage with the department of civil engineering that allows students to take a package of courses in the transportation area. The program has been adding more small business/entrepreneurship courses to the program. As for functional areas, there have been complaints about the marketing classes. "The marketing area really lacks a lot. They're small and don't have a lot of focus," says one. The exception is international marketing, which students uniformly praise.

The small size of the program means a smaller selection of electives. Courses that are undersubscribed tend to get dropped. "We would like to offer more electives," says Betts, "but when you're small you can't get the diversity in courses."

Students complain that the program is too theoretical, but Betts claims that as alumni they come to value the education. "It forces a way of thinking. We can all think back to the teacher in high school that we complained about but came to appreciate."

Living It Up

On campus, students hang out in the business lounge and the computer lab. Everyone goes to the campus pubs, The Social Club and The Cellar. The Lunar Rogue Pub in town is popular with some students. The main student club is the MBA Society, which organizes orientation for new students and sends people to business conferences. It's also in charge of the yearly International Night.

The Payoff

Recruiting is a major weakness at the MBA level. "Nobody comes to talk specifically to MBA students at UNB," a student says. MBAs do have access to the central career centre on campus and can apply for any jobs that turn up there. There is no tracking of grads, though estimates have it that 80% of grads are employed within six months of graduation.

The Bottom Line

Foreign Affairs

There are two MBA exchanges with universities in Belgium and France; four more in France, Mexico, Chile, and the US are being negotiated.

Money for Nothing

There are three scholarships available to MBA students, ranging in value from $3,000 to $5,000. Most second-year students work as teaching or research assistants at a salary of $1,500 to $2,000 per year.

Other Options

Joint MBA/LLB

Contacts

Faculty of Administration • University of New Brunswick • PO Box 4400 • Fredericton, NB • E3B 5A3 • (506) 453-4869 • www.fadmin.unb.ca

UNIVERSITY OF NEW BRUNSWICK, FREDERICTON— VITAL STATISTICS	
total university enrollment	8,905
total full-time undergrad enrollment	6,800
number of full-time professors in the faculty of administration	37
number of part-time professors	N/A
number of women professors	7 full-time

MBA

full-time enrollment	58
part-time enrollment	53
size of entering class	30
women students	46%
out-of-province students	30%
international students	10%
students straight from undergrad	10%
average age	28
annual tuition	$3,423
annual tuition for international students	$5,723
length of program	2 years
number of applications	200
number of acceptances	40
cut-off grade for admission	3.0 out of 4.0
average grade of admittees	3.3
average GMAT	550
years of work experience required	3 preferred
average years of work experience	5
size of core classes	25
size of electives	25
classes taught by full-time faculty	100%
grads employed within six months of graduation	no formal tracking

University of New Brunswick— Saint John

Even though the University of New Brunswick's Saint John campus is an adjunct to the main campus in Fredericton, its business school has managed to carve out a niche for itself. The school offers the only one-year MBA in the Maritimes and is one of two MBAs in Canada to have branched out into the field of electronic commerce.

In autumn of 1997 the first students started in UNBSJ's new one-year MBA with a focus on international business. The program aims to raise the profile of the Saint John campus. "We work very closely with the business community in our city and they wanted that international focus," says John Chalykoff, dean of the school. The plan is to have eventually a foreign student population of at least 50% in the program. As well, a number of professors have international experience and backgrounds, particularly in Eastern Europe. Students entering in autumn of 1999 will also be able to take a specialization in electronic commerce.

Though students at the Fredericton campus malign Saint John, the natural setting of UNBSJ is lovely. ("They're always saying that Saint John smells bad because of the pulp and paper companies," scoffs a UNBSJ student. "But Fredericton is so small that it would fit easily inside the clean part of Saint John.") The 1965 campus is on a ridge that looks down over the Saint John river valley. The business school is in its own spanking new building, a 10-minute car ride from the city centre.

MBA

Getting In

The faculty received 57 applications for entry to the second class of the new program. Twenty-eight students were admitted. The program requires students to have a four-year undergraduate degree, two years of relevant work experience, and acceptable GMAT scores. The minimum average for admission is 3.0 out of 4.0, and the average is a 3.6. There is no foreign language requirement. "Not that we shouldn't attempt to learn other languages, it's just that English is the language of business," says Chalykoff. Any foreign student who has a TOEFL result under 550 will be required to attend a three-month language module before the start of the program.

Profs, Programs, and Particulars

The MBA is divided into four eight-week course modules: business basics, managing business functions, industry analysis and business competitiveness, and a choice between international business and electronic commerce. Besides the courses, the other elements of the curriculum are special topic seminars that might deal with such issues as NAFTA and the Canadian economy. A course on "individual effectiveness" (yes, terminology has been taken from a large tub of jargon) runs year long, teaching interpersonal skills, computer skills, and communication skills. Workshops scattered throughout the program help students integrate what they have learned in their regular courses.

Between the third and fourth modules, students go on a mandatory 12-week internship. Foreign students are guaranteed a position in a Canadian company, and domestic students are guaranteed a similar one abroad. So far Canadian students have been placed in internships in China, Germany, Indonesia, Poland, and Uruguay, and foreign students have taken jobs in Florenceville, Saint John, and Toronto.

The Payoff

UNBSJ's MBA produced its first grads in 1998. The MBA administrators have been working with the campus career centre, sending out student CVs to employment agencies and companies that inquire after grads. At present there are no hard statistics on what happens to students after graduation.

The Bottom Line

Foreign Affairs

The faculty is in the process of negotiating its first international exchange with a university in Hong Kong.

Money for Nothing

The school awards two full-time scholarships, one worth $9,000 and the other worth $18,000. No students are employed as TAs or research assistants.

Contacts

Faculty of Business • University of New Brunswick • PO Box 5050 • Saint John, NB • E2L 4L5 • (506) 648-5570 • business.unbsj.ca/bba/

UNIVERSITY OF NEW BRUNSWICK, SAINT JOHN— VITAL STATISTICS

total university enrollment	3,029
total full-time undergrad enrollment	1,996
number of full-time professors in the faculty of business	18
number of part-time professors	20
number of women professors	6 full-time

MBA

full-time enrollment	18
part-time enrollment	50
size of entering class	30 (18 full-time, 12 part-time)
women students	25%
out-of-province students	40%
international students	50%
students straight from undergrad	1
total tuition	$18,000
total tuition for international students	same
number of applications	57
number of acceptances	28
cut-off grade for admission	3.0 out of 4.0
average grade of admittees	3.6
average GMAT	580
years of work experience required	2
average years of work experience	10
size of core classes	18 to 25
size of electives	N/A
classes taught by full-time faculty	95%
grads employed six months after graduation	not tracked

University of Ottawa

The University of Ottawa should have a glowing reputation. It's in the centre of power and political intrigue, and it's next door to Silicon Valley North, the highest concentration of high-tech firms in Canada. Instead, the university is filled with students who say, "The programs are fabulous," but add, "they're much better than people think they are."

Ottawa U certainly doesn't have a bad reputation, it just doesn't have any reputation at all. One Ottawa resident even claims not to have known of the institution's existence until it was time to fill out university applications. Part of the problem is that the programs draw mainly from their immediate surroundings. "It's a Catch 22. We think it's a regional program and as a regional program we think it must not be as good," says an MBA student.

Ottawa's Faculty of Administration offers an MBA, an International MBA, and an Executive MBA. If there's one program where being regional is an asset rather than a liability, it's the Executive MBA. Ottawa's EMBA competes with Queen's National Executive MBA, which is also located in downtown

Ottawa. By dint of making life easier for participants, Ottawa has been holding its own against Queen's. (This is particularly satisfying because much of the moaning at the undergrad level centres on Queen's and its reputation.)

> Like most things in the capital, Ottawa U is bilingual. One of the best things about the place is that you can come out of it speaking both French and English, says an anglo administrator, who proceeds to admit that he himself is largely unilingual. Every course is taught twice, once in French and once in English, so that, in theory, you can simply choose the better professor. (Though this doesn't happen all that often.) Students can also submit papers and exams in either language.

The University of Ottawa has a large sprawling concrete campus in downtown Ottawa. The Rideau Canal is right by the school and students can skate to class in winter. Business has an older building to itself, described by one MBA as "slightly decrepit."

MBA

Getting In

In 1997-98 the MBA received 725 applications and sent out 250 acceptances. The minimum grade for admission is a B, and the average of admitted students is a B+. Two years of work experience are strongly preferred. No longer will B.Comms be able to go straight from the undergrad into the MBA.

Atmospherics

The atmosphere in the program varies greatly with the year. The class of 1996 was a pugnacious close-knit group made up of slightly older students. But usually the class tends to break up into two clusters: older people with lots of work experience and a very young crowd of people without work experience.

Most people in the MBA program are bilingual and those in the IMBA are required to be so. The IMBA has large numbers of international students, one of the best things about the program.

Profs, Programs, and Particulars

Since September 1997, the MBA has been a 15-month program with modules, professional development, new specializations, and a major project. All students, including part-timers, will be admitted to a cohort. Courses are taught as six-week modules with exams after each module. The largest part of the program is taken up by the core, which is taught in an integrated fashion. All core courses are taught in French and English and applicants to the program need to specify on their application form which language stream they want.

> The new program offers concentrations in finance, governance, high technology, international management, and marketing. Students who choose not to specialize take the option in general management. Specialization courses are taught in both languages, and students may pick and choose as they see fit.

The project is optional for students with lots of work experience. It is completed during the final stages of the program and will probably require students to engage in field research. There's also the option of writing a thesis instead. But anyone who has less than two years of experience must complete the project.

All students participate in two skills development modules, one at the beginning of the program and the other midway through. These cover everything from group work to negotiations.

> ### International MBA
>
> Students in the International MBA complete the same core as the regular MBA students and then apply to enter the IMBA. All IMBA courses are compulsory. In addition to functional areas such as international marketing, students also take courses in areas such as multinational logistics and manufacturing and international information systems management. A major part of the IMBA is the three-month internship that students may complete in Canada or abroad. Since the program's beginning, students have worked in more than 20 countries.

Living It Up

The MBAs have their own lounge on the fourth floor, "but undergrads flowed into the MBA space," complains one student. Some MBAs go to the Nox, though it's more of an undergrad hangout. Off campus, Fathers and Sons is the hands-down favourite place because the MBA Society has a deal with the establishment for drink specials. Another off-campus hangout is the Royal Oak. The MBA Society is the principal MBA club.

The Payoff

MBAs have access to the same services as undergrads. The career services office tracked down 66 out of 195 grads of the class of 1997, and found that within a year 95% of them had found employment at an average base starting salary of $55,568.

> ### A-list Alumni
>
> - Rhonda St. Croix MBA '91: Vice-President, Regulatory and Planning, ACC TelEnterprises Ltd.
> - Tom Trottier MBA '87: President, Information Animation, Ottawa
> - Jacques Goupil MBA '84: Chairman and CEO, Auberges des Gouverneurs Inc. and President, Maxrelco Inc., Montreal

- Richard Bertrand MBA '82: Vice-President, Marketing, SHL Systemhouse Inc.
- Kiran Kulkarni MBA '74: President, Security Information Systems, Brampton, ON

Executive MBA

The EMBA was founded in 1992 and is run with the university's seven corporate partners: Bell Canada, Canada Post Corp., The Perez Group, Canada Trust, Toshiba of Canada Ltd., Nova Network, and Microsoft Canada. The partners provide support with infrastructure and facilities; Ottawa U provides a program for partners' employees.

Applicants need a minimum of five years' relevant work experience and those admitted usually have closer to 15. About a third of participants come from the public sector, two-thirds from the private sector. English is the language of instruction, though students may submit papers, give presentations, and take exams in French.

The EMBA is predicated on making life easier for participants. Classes are held in the World Exchange Plaza in downtown Ottawa. Participants get several perks, including a laptop computer, meals on class days, indoor parking in the building, access to a local golf course, and membership at Le Club Universitaire, a tony Ottawa club. In addition, instructors are available around the clock. "I'm here most evenings. My family doesn't see that much of me but the participants do," says André deCarufel, director of the EMBA.

Despite its presence in the capital, the program is geared more toward the private sector than the public. Before the program starts, there's a boot camp for those who lack math and computer skills. All material is taught in an integrated fashion. The EMBA has a focus on international management. Several courses deal with multinational management and there's a study abroad trip, which has sent students to Chile, Hong Kong, and Malaysia in the past. All participants must complete an independent research project.

The Bottom Line

Foreign Affairs

The faculty has an impressive 35 exchange agreements with universities in Australia, Denmark, England, France, Norway, Thailand, the Netherlands, the US, Sweden, and Mexico.

Money for Nothing

The faculty does not offer scholarships to MBAs. Instead there is a lump sum of money that all grad students at the university compete for. In 1996-97, 12 MBAs received scholarships, ranging in value from $1,500 to $2,000. Students may also work as graders or research assistants. Graders earn $12 an hour; RAs earn $25.

Options

- Joint MBA/LLB
- Joint MBA/LLL
- Master in engineering management
- Master in health administration
- Master in systems science

Contacts

Faculty of Administration • University of Ottawa • 136 Jean Jacques Lussier St. • Ottawa, ON • K1N 6N5 • (613) 562-5731 • www.uottawa.ca/academic/adm

UNIVERSITY OF OTTAWA—VITAL STATISTICS

total university enrollment	22,695
total full-time undergrad enrollment	14,137
number of full-time professors in the faculty of administration	73
number of part-time professors	45
number of women professors	5 full-time

MBA

full-time enrollment	184
part-time enrollment	328
size of entering class	82 full-time; 84 part-time
women students	43%
out-of-province students	25%
international students	10%
students straight from undergrad	10%
average age	29 full-time; 33 part-time
tuition	$1,912 per term
tuition for international students	$3,630 per term
length of program	15 months
number of applications	725
number of acceptances	250
cut-off grade for admission	B
average grade of admittees	B+
average GMAT	573
years of work experience required	2
average years of work experience	5.5

size of core classes	40
size of electives	20
classes taught by full-time faculty	82%
grads employed full-time within a year of graduation	95%
number of postings	645 (includes B.Comm)
grads hired through placement office	20%
average starting salary	$55,568
what employment figures are based on	66 out of 195 grads of the class of 1997

Executive MBA

enrollment	209
women students	23%
average age	40
average GMAT	N/A
years of work experience required	5
average years of work experience	15
cost of program	$38,500

Université du Québec à Montréal

The École des Sciences de la Gestion (ESG) at the Université du Québec à Montréal is to the École des Hautes Études Commerciales (HEC) as Concordia is to McGill: young, energetic, and in the shadow of its more illustrious predecessor. But no one really cares. "We have a lot less prestige, but we're not shy about it. We laugh about it," says an MBA student. "Besides if you look at *l'Actualité*, they now say that the future in business is at UQAM."

The ESG is a huge school. It has four departments: economics, urban and tourism studies, accounting, and management, which offers an MBA, an Executive MBA, an MBA in Financial Services, an MBA in Real Estate Management, and a PhD (given jointly with McGill, HEC, and Concordia), as well as a slew of undergraduate business programs. Lots of UQAM professors do consulting work, to the point that "the administration can have trouble knowing where the professors are," says Léon-Michel Serruya, director of the EMBA and the MBA in Financial Services. The school has also been extending its reach worldwide: a version of the EMBA is now available in six foreign countries.

UQAM is in the centre of the Latin Quarter of Montreal, a dynamic student area filled with cafés and equal parts of sleaze and class. When the university was founded in 1968, it rented buildings and bought them as it had the cash. It renovated some of the old buildings in the area, preserving the façade while gutting the inside. These buildings are among the most elegant of the district and some of the renovations have been awarded prizes. The ESG is in a brand new building, which looks out on an inner courtyard.

MBA

Getting In

UQAM's MBA is really a Master of Science with a more marketable title. For this reason, all applicants need an undergraduate degree in business. You apply directly for the specialization you want to enter. In 1996-97, the program received 276 applications of which it accepted 115. Some specializations have admission quotas because of greater demand. Finance, marketing, and international business are particularly popular. You need a minimum average of 3.2 out of 4.3 to be considered. The average grade varies with the specialization chosen. No work experience is required.

Recently the program has instituted a system of rolling admissions whereby a candidate's file is evaluated as soon as it's received and admissions take place all year long.

Atmospherics

The MBA student body is a cohesive group of about 60 students. "The atmosphere is really good. We all help each other out," says a student. There's a sense of students having emerged from the scrum of undergrad. In certain years, the students have been quite competitive with lots of academic achievers vying for good grades. Ninety-nine percent of students come straight from undergrad. No one studies part-time, and a large proportion of students took their undergrad in business at

UQAM. People are divided into their areas of specialization, so aside from two or three common classes with 60 people in them, most classes have only about 10 students.

Profs, Programs, and Particulars

If you enroll in UQAM's MBA program you'll emerge a specialist, not a manager. The program consists of three parts: a core that is common to all specializations, five specialization courses, and a thesis, which students spend most of second year writing. The core consists of only two classes: strategic management and the environment of the firm.

> UQAM offers specializations in the following areas: real estate, strategy, marketing, decision technologies, organizational development, management, industrial relations and personnel, international business, quality and re-engineering, and finance. There is talk of adding a specialization in transportation.

Students say the quality of teaching is high. The most valuable part of the education is the thesis, which is often a work of applied research. Most advisers work closely with their students, who come out with strong analytical skills. Students come in without work experience and leave without it as well. Says a student, "Most of the jobs that require experience are management jobs, which we're not trained for anyway." Most courses require at least one major presentation.

Living It Up

There are numerous student cafés in the area, such as the Café Internet, Van Houtte's, and the Second Cup. Nearby St. Denis Street is home to many Thai and Vietnamese restaurants.

The main student club is the MBA Association. Its primary job is to represent MBA students at UQAM. MBAs can also participate in the undergraduate clubs. The most popular of these are AIESEC and the Marketing Club. Students can get experience with local businesses through BIG, the small business consulting group.

The Payoff

Students find jobs in a variety of ways: professors' contacts; companies they've worked on in their thesis; personal contacts; and last and least, through the general career placement office. "It isn't very good," says one student. "Most of the jobs are for beginners." The school does not keep regular employment figures. For what it's worth, a survey of students who graduated between 1987 and 1993 showed that 56% had jobs within six months of graduation at an average salary of $45,000. The rate of response to the survey is not known. About 20% of students go on to do a PhD.

> **A-list Alumni**
>
> - Serge Rémillard MBA '87: Senior Vice-President, Administration and Control, Caisse de dépôt et placement du Québec
> - Louise Champoux-Paillé MBA '87: Executive Vice-President and Director General, Ordre des administrateurs agréés du Québec
> - Réal Raymond MBA '86: Senior Vice-President, Treasury and Financial Markets, National Bank of Canada

MBA in Financial Services

In 1996 UQAM began offering an MBA in financial services in conjunction with the Institute of Canadian Bankers (ICB). The financial services industry is a natural fit for ESG. The industry is the biggest employer in Montreal, and many professors have taught for the ICB and developed course materials for them. This program is offered in both Quebec City and Montreal.

All courses are taught by UQAM professors using ICB copyrighted materials. Students choose a specialization in one of five areas: personal financial planning, portfolio and investment management, management of treasury risks, small business, and personal trusts. The eight courses in the common core are taught live; the specialized courses are available partly through videos and correspondence.

MBA in Real Estate Management

In 1998 UQAM accepted its first class to the new MBA in real estate management, a natural addition to the faculty, since that area of study was already available in the regular MBA. Students spend every third Friday, Saturday, and Sunday in the program for a total program length of two years. Everyone must complete 13 courses ranging in topic from socioeconmic and urban contexts, to strategic real estate management and planning and project management. The program started off with 30 recruits, among them startling numbers of accountants and lawyers.

Executive MBA

UQAM used to offer the only full-time Executive MBA in Canada. When the program started, nearly 20 years ago, it attracted people who had taken a leave of absence from their jobs but recently administrators realized that they were losing students who couldn't afford to give up their job. The only option now available is a part-time one. A version of this program is also delivered in Témiscamingue, Quebec, and in Poland, Ecuador, Algeria, Vietnam, Morocco, and the Dominican Republic. Plans are underway for this program to be given in France, Chile, and Tunisia as well.

Students have a minimum of 22 months in which to complete the program and a maximum of four years. Most participants are in their late 30s with about 10 years' work experience.

The program is geared toward general management and has two strong points: the integration of different disciplines and group work. Groups are assigned randomly by the administrators. The five basic blocks that students go through in the program include: the manager and the firm, commercial and financial management, management of operations and goods and services, strategic management, and international management.

The Bottom Line

Foreign Affairs

The ESG has exchanges with about 18 universities in France, the Netherlands, England, Germany, Mexico, and the US. The school is a member of the US-based Institute of International Education, which gives students access to an additional seven or eight universities in the US and Mexico.

Money for Nothing

MBAs are eligible for 31 scholarships, ranging in value from $500 to $15,000. About 60 students work as teaching assistants; six work as research assistants; and 20 are employed as lecturers. TAs earn between $11 and $12.50 an hour.

Other Options

- Master in Project Management
- Master in Urban Analysis and Management
- Master in Computer Management
- Master in Accounting
- PhD

Contacts

École des Sciences de la Gestion • Université du Québec à Montréal • Case Postale 6192, Succursale Centre-Ville • Montréal, QC • H3C 4R2 • (514) 987-6852 • www.regis.uqam.ca/index_pgm/sciences_gestion.html

UNIVERSITÉ DU QUÉBEC À MONTRÉAL—VITAL STATISTICS

total university enrollment	38,510
total full-time undergrad enrollment	34,010
number of full-time professors in the management department	96
number of part-time professors	92
number of women professors	21

MBA

full-time enrollment	153
part-time enrollment	none
size of entering class	56
women students	44%
out-of-province students	N/A
international students	15%
students straight from undergrad	99%
average age	24
tuition for Quebec students	$166 per course
tuition for Canadian students	$166 per course
tuition for international students	$826 per course
length of program	2 years
number of applications	276
number of acceptances	115
cut-off grade for admission	3.2 out of 4.3
average grade of admittees	3.2+
average GMAT	not required
years of work experience required	none
average years of work experience	N/A

size of core classes	56
size of electives	1 to 15
classes taught by full-time faculty	100%
grads employed within six months of graduation	56%
number of on-campus recruiters	5
grads hired through placement office	N/A
average starting salary	$45,000
what employment figures are based on	survey of students graduating between 1987 and 1993

MBA in Financial Services
(figures include all sites where the program is given)

enrollment	232
women students	87
average age	42
average GMAT	not required
years of work experience required	4
average years of work experience	12
cost of program	$9,030

Executive MBA
(figures include all sites where the program is given)

enrollment	322
women students	113
average age	37
average GMAT	not required
years of work experience required	4
average years of work experience	10
cost of program	$4,200

Queen's University

In the mid-nineties Queen's School of Business undertook a daring experiment. After assessing the old MBA as good-but-not-great, faculty members banded together to come up with a new direction for the program. With the full support of the university, they laid the groundwork for an MBA that was unusual in several ways. The program focussed on the niche market of science and technology; it was one year in length; and it functioned independently of government support.

The MBA enrolled its first students in 1996, and three years later has fully delivered on its promises. Numerous science grads have been able to enter the ranks of management while remaining in their scientific field. The niche marketing has attracted foreign students who in many cases have applied to no other Canadian MBA program. And Queen's starting salaries for MBA grads are now among the highest in Canada. (In many cases, grads have taken jobs that pay at least twice as much as their pre-MBA jobs.)

The school has been daring in other ways. In 1996 it hired a new dean, Margot Northey, and inaugurated several firsts in the school. Northey is the first business dean not already from Queen's; her previous position was at Queen's arch-rival, the Richard Ivey School of Business at Western; she has an oddball background (her PhD is in Canadian lit and she came to business via management communications); and she is a woman. "I think it's a credit to the school that they did choose me," says Northey.

Queen's handsome limestone campus dates from 1841. The business school is in the neat but not glamorous Dunning Hall. By contrast, the MBA facility, located in the basement of Dunning Hall, feels a bit like a high-tech bunker. The space has been conceived of as carefully as any operations problem set: students send questions to their professors by e-mail; offices are proximate so that students don't waste any seconds getting to the classroom; notes on the monitor at the front of the superclassroom download automatically to the students' laptops. It's all part of an effort to emulate the workplace as much as possible.

MBA

Getting In

Queen's received 300 applications for entry to the third class of its Science and Technology MBA and accepted 88 of those. The cut-off grade is 3.0 out of 4.0 and the average grade of admitted students is 3.3. On paper you need two to three years of work experience, some of it managerial, and an undergraduate degree in health science, science, engineering, mathematics, or computer science. (Twenty percent of those who started in September 1998 already had a doctorate.) But there is some leeway in these requirements.

> Applicants who have everything but the work experience can take part in a 16-month internship with Celestica Inc., after which they may enter the program. The science degree requirement can be waived provided a student has gotten the background some other way—the MBA director's favourite example is a hypothetical daughter of Bill Gates with a literature degree. You need a science background for two reasons: to keep up with the material and because "the science and technology industry said to us: 'You can't work in our industry unless you can talk to our clients,'" says Ken Wong, former chair of the program.

Admissions is a tripartite process designed to ensure that admittees are wireheads with hearts. Stage one weeds out people without the academic background. Stage two reviews the essays and the applicant's character. ("I don't want to spend time convincing people that other people matter," says Wong.) By stage three, the evaluation is over and it's a question of how well the applicant fits in with the rest of the class.

Atmospherics

The class is small, just 60 people, and there is a close bond between students in the program. Students are divided into teams of five or six at the beginning of the program. Each team has its own office—a slit of a room with the students' names on the door—and a faculty mentor who also acts as an intermediary.

It's part of the program's mission to be as responsive as possible to students. The program director regularly hauls all the students into the boardroom to ask for feedback on the program. In such matters as the income-contingent bank loan (see Money for Nothing), administrators have been quick to pounce on the phone whenever students have problems with the bank.

In the land of the quants, who are the poets? "They all have the souls of poets," claims Wong. "Other programs' non-quants are down here," says one former engineer, patting the floor. "When we talk about non-quant, we're talking here," raising her hand to chin-level. It's probably a bit easier if you have a background in a hard science, but even engineers who've been out of school for a decade can struggle taking a derivative. Engineers, who make up about half the student body, have another advantage: "I was used to not getting the right answer and to that feeling of uncertainty and anxiety," says an engineer from Nortel.

In the old program, women represented about 35% of the student body. In the new program, that figure is down to 20%, but Wong expects the numbers to rise as the program matures.

A-list Alumni

- John See MBA '81: President and Chief Operating Officer, TD Waterhouse Securities Inc.
- Dee Parkinson MBA '76: Executive Vice-President, Oil Sands Group of Suncor, Fort McMurray, Alta.
- Paul Gagné MBA '75: President and CEO, Avenor Inc.; Chairman of the Board of Directors, The Canadian Pulp and Paper Association
- James William Leech MBA '73: President and CEO, Disys Corp., Mississauga, Ont.
- David Radler MBA '67: President, Hollinger Inc., Vancouver

Profs, Programs, and Particulars

The first of the four 10-week phases in the program brings people up to speed in basics such as managerial economics. But because everyone has a technical background, there's no need to spend time on remedial stats. The second phase teaches the functional areas in an integrated fashion. Phase three deals with the strategic management of science and technology companies. In phase four, students choose to specialize in finance, marketing, or operations and information technology, and they take part in a five-week corporate internship.

The goal of the internship is to give students a taste of project management. This is one of the few times that students aren't required to work in groups, since companies that have sponsored a student's enrollment in the MBA may get their employee to complete a short project for them. Projects could involve anything from writing a business plan for a biotechnology company to evaluating a smart card venture between a municipal government and the banks.

> Each program phase is preceded by a week-long professional development program that teaches everything from team work and job search techniques to the management of diversity and proper corporate citizenship. There is even a short session on table manners to ensure that students know which fork to use at fancy dinners.

To prepare faculty for teaching the management of science and technology, Wong set aside $250,000 for course development and sent professors off to conferences. But the program also makes use of a virtual faculty. When the program lacks expertise in-house, they beam in experts through the videoconference apparatus.

Could you graduate from the program and make a career selling potato chips rather than computer chips? It would be perverse but you probably could. "They really don't compromise the business side," says one student. But as another points out, "It's pretty hard to avoid high technology."

Living It Up

The work is intense but students do manage to take some time off. Four members of the first MBA class even joined a Kingston hockey league and contrived to play 47 games while they were in the program. There are regular outings on Thursday night to the Grizzly Grill, a restaurant with a bar, a dance floor, and pool tables. The main on-campus hangout is the Grad Club. And whenever any student has a party, e-mail invitations go out to every member of the MBA class.

By design, there is no MBA Association. "We'd been learning all about the leaderless work environment and we thought we'd try it out to see if it worked," says a student. Whenever something such as a Christmas party or a trip to the MBA Games needs to be planned, an ad hoc committee forms to deal with it.

The Payoff

The MBA has a career manager who is there to generate opportunities for students. "This program has a performance guarantee. We are putting an emphasis on the fact that people will get jobs," says career manager Catherine Purcell. Purcell persuades companies that have never recruited at Queen's in the past to take a look at the students.

Though the focus of the new MBA is narrower than that of the old, roughly the same number of companies are coming on campus. High-tech firms such as Newbridge Networks Corp. show up, but so do more mainstream companies with high-tech divisions. PricewaterhouseCoopers used to come to recruit accounting students, now it shows up to recruit for its information systems division. Eighty percent of students from the class of 1998 were employed at graduation at an average starting salary of $75,000.

The National Executive MBA and the Executive MBA in Ottawa

Queen's school of business offers two Executive MBAs with identical curricula and faculty. The only difference is in the mode of delivery. The EMBA in Ottawa is offered live by Queen's profs who make the trek to Ottawa every two weeks. The National EMBA is offered via videoconferencing in 23 sites in Canada and one in Bermuda.

Admissions requirements are the same for both programs. Participants need a minimum of eight years of managerial experience; most have almost twice that. A few applicants who lack an undergraduate degree may be admitted to the program. Students may take either the GMAT or the QMAT, a similar test designed for Queen's by New York-based Kaplan Educational Centers. EMBA and NEMBA classes take place all day Friday and Saturday every other week.

Students in all programs take a total of 23 courses between August and May over two years. At the beginning of the program everyone spends a two-week summer term at Queen's for sessions on marketing and communications, leadership, and health and lifestyle (read: how not to stress out too much during the program). There's a similar session at the beginning of second year. Students work on two management research projects throughout the program.

> While the programs are identical, the difference in mode of delivery makes for a completely different class dynamic. In the videoconferencing program you get a cross-national perspective from the other students that you don't get from the Ottawa class.

Here's how the videoconferencing class works. Students sit at a table with two TV screens in front of them. One shows the prof lecturing in Kingston; the other shows whatever site your classmate is talking from. Every student has a personal key pad. You press one button to identify yourself and ask a question, another to signal anonymously that you don't understand and could the prof slow down a bit. The prof can't hear what's going on at a site unless you buzz her or she buzzes your site. This means that students at a site can have a discreet conversation if someone needs something explained.

How does Queen's videoconference MBA differ from Western's? In Western's program, the groups are larger per site and students sit in tiered rows. When they break up into smaller groups for outside projects, they can actually choose who they're going to be with. At Queen's Toronto site, students are eight to a rowboat-shaped table, like rowers in a galley ship. You spend two years with the same bunch of people, and the group feels much closer than at Western.

The biggest difference is that the Queen's prof can't see all 24 screens at once. This allows for more levity at Queen's, though there's no doubt that Western's feels more proper. During a slow moment in a Saturday afternoon lecture, a Queen's participant whips out a thick felt marker and outlines the prof's face on the TV screen. Everyone laughs uproariously each time the professor moves his head vigorously enough to stray outside the outline.

The Bottom Line

Foreign Affairs

There are no international exchanges in the MBA program.

Money for Nothing

The MBA has the highest fees this side of Executive MBAs. To keep the program accessible, the school has an agreement with the Royal Bank to offer income-contingent loans that are payable only when the grad hits a salary of more than $50,000. Along with the loan, you also get a number of perks like a Gold Visa Card and the services of a personal banker.

Options

- Master of science in management
- PhD

Contacts

Queen's School of Business • Queen's University • Kingston, ON • K7L 3N6 • (613) 545-2330 • business.queensu.ca

QUEEN'S UNIVERSITY—VITAL STATISTICS	
total university enrollment	16,500
total full-time undergrad enrollment	11,000
number of full-time professors in the school of business	53
number of part-time professors	17
number of women professors	12
MBA	
full-time enrollment	60
part-time enrollment	none
size of entering class	60
women students	20%
out-of-province students	30%
international students	10%
students straight from undergrad	none
average age	30
total tuition and fees	$26,500
total tuition and fees for international students	$26,500

length of program	1 year
number of applications	300
number of acceptances	88
cut-off grade for admission	3.0 out of 4.0
average grade of admittees	3.3
average GMAT	648
years of work experience required	2 to 3
average years of work experience	6
size of core classes	60
size of electives	20
classes taught by full-time faculty	70%
grads employed at graduation	80%
number of on-campus recruiters	210
grads hired through placement office	N/A
average starting salary	$75,000
what employment figures are based on	100% of class of '98

Executive MBA in Ottawa

enrollment	103
women students	30%
average age	38
years of work experience required	8
average years of work experience	15
cost of program	$49,000

National Executive MBA

enrollment	315
women students	26%
average age	38
years of work experience required	8
average years of work experience	15
cost of program	$57,000

University of Regina

The big advantage of the University of Regina's MBA program is that it exists at all, since this is only program that Regina professionals have access to, aside from pricey distance EMBAs. "In most schools, part-time students are secondary to full-time students. But our program is really focused on the part-time people," says Jack Ito, director of the MBA.

But it can be hard to be a have-not university in a have-not province. A few years ago there was talk of shutting down the U of R and amalgamating it with the University of Saskatchewan. In 1993 a provincial inquiry decided that, for the time being, there was room for two universities in Saskatchewan and that they should try not to duplicate each other's programs.

The U of R is located on the outskirts of Regina. The campus looks its age: the university was established in 1974 and many of the block-like buildings are of that vintage. Underfunding doesn't make the campus look any better. Admin shares a building with engineering and education.

MBA

Getting In

Most MBA students are working professionals from the Regina area with about 10 years of work experience. In fact, students from outside Southern Saskatchewan are usually turned away, though this policy is under review. There is no entering year as such, but the faculty received 44 applications most recently and accepted 24 of these. The minimum average for admission is 70%. Applicants need two years' work experience, but the MBA also accepts students who have just completed an undergrad degree and are working at a first job. Students with an average of less than 70% can take makeup courses.

Atmospherics

Students say the best thing about the program is the contact with other students. "People will say, 'In our organization we do such and such.' And because it's fairly small, you do recognize most of the people," says an alumnus. There is strong representation from government and Crown corporations. A number of students are from the banking and insurance industries and from local companies such as Wascana. All classes are held in the evenings and on weekends.

Profs, Programs, and Particulars

In 1995, U of R took its small master of administration program, which offered options in business management and public policy/administration, and split it into two: an MBA and an MPA. The MBA is geared toward general management, and there are no specializations. The first-year curriculum consists of eight required qualifying classes, but many students get exemptions. So far, many of these required courses have been undergraduate admin courses, but the faculty plans to offer special graduate qualifying courses that will be limited to 25 people.

In second year, students take two required courses and eight electives or six electives with a project. Though there aren't any specializations, it's possible for MBA students to take several courses on the public side. There is a cluster of courses in the management process area that includes topics such as entrepreneurship, change management, and total quality management. Courses have been added in the areas of international business and human resources management.

Living It Up

After night classes, students will sometimes head off to P.J. Millers, a local pub. Some students participate in the University of Regina Alumni Classic Golf Tournament. The faculty hosts the occasional wine and cheese for students.

The Payoff

Most students come into the program already employed. There are no statistics on the handful of full-time students.

The Bottom Line

Foreign Affairs

The faculty of administration does not have any international exchanges.

Money for Nothing

There are three graduate scholarships for MBA students with values of $1,000 to $6,000. At present two students work as TAs but the number varies with the number of full-time grad students. TAs earn $3,518 per semester.

Other Options

- Master of Public Administration
- Master of Human Resources Management

Contacts

Faculty of Administration • University of Regina • Education Building • Regina, SK • S4S 0A2 • (306) 585-4724 • www.uregina.ca/admin/

UNIVERSITY OF REGINA—VITAL STATISTICS

total university enrollment	10,811
total full-time undergrad enrollment	7,416
number of full-time professors in the faculty of administration	23
number of part-time professors	8
number of women professors	5
MBA	
full-time enrollment	5
part-time enrollment	63
women students	41%
out-of-province students	none
international students	2
students straight from undergrad	none
average age	32
tuition	$600 per course
tuition for international students	same

length of program	2 years
number of applications	44
number of acceptances	24
cut-off grade for admission	70%
average grade of admittees	B+
average GMAT	N/A
years of work experience required	2
average years of work experience	10
size of core classes	60 to 100
size of electives	25
classes taught by full-time faculty	95%
grads employed within six months of graduation	most students are already employed

Royal Roads University

From its inception in 1996, Royal Roads in Victoria has been an experiment in education. When the university started its commerce program, it admitted students with two years of college and allowed them to complete third and fourth-year in a single year. But it also accepted substantial work experience as a pre-requisite, in effect enabling someone with no education past high school to get a university degree in 12 months. "We're creating access and taking away barriers," says a former administrator.

Royal Roads prides itself on programs that are more practical and relevant than what's offered at a traditional university. "The prof doesn't say, 'In theory, this is what should happen.' He says, 'This is what happened,'" says a student. The university has four divisions: conflict management, environmental management, leadership, and business management, which has offered a part-time executive style MBA program since 1999. The MBA has four streams: executive management, digital technologies, human resources management, and public relations and communications—a first for a Canadian MBA program and one that has stretched the definition of an MBA program.

Royal Roads is on the spacious grounds of the former Royal Roads Military College, overlooking the ocean. (The university is leasing the buildings and has no connection with the defunct college.) The focal point of campus life is Hatley House, a small turreted castle with a luxurious interior, built in 1908 for James Dunsmuir, a mining magnate and former BC premier. A flock of peacocks and miniature deer make their home on campus.

MBA

Getting in

Royal Roads' MBA admits mid-career professionals with seven to ten years of work experience. The university will accept students without an undergraduate degree, and applicants are not required to take the GMAT.

Profs, Program, and Particulars

The MBA program has three residency periods of three weeks each, seven courses delivered through distance education, and an organizational consulting project. The entire program takes two years to complete. The distance portions of the program are delivered through a variety of methods such as Internet, correspondence, and videotape. Students may complete the consulting project in their own organization.

The Bottom Line

Foreign Affairs
There are no international exchanges for MBA students.

Money for Nothing
Royal Roads University offers eight MBA Entrance Awards of $1,000. These are awarded on the basis of academic merit and a personal essay.

Contacts
Management Programs Division • Royal Roads University • 2005 Sooke Rd. • Victoria, BC • V9B 5Y2 • (250) 391-2626•
www.royalroads.ca/bcomem

Saint Mary's University

Saint Mary's University is just like home. But it's a home where no one is ever rude or nasty; people preach the values of community and inclusiveness; and football is part of the glue that binds everyone together. "People are here to get the best education they can without killing each other," says an MBA student.

The Frank E. Sobey School of Commerce is the pride and joy of this smallish Halifax university, founded in 1802. If you're from the Maritimes and have been business-bound since tothood, SMU (that's "smew") is probably the first place you considered. Frequent comment: "I wanted to stay local and from what everyone said, this was the best business school in the Maritimes."

> At SMU you'll find a large business school in a small university setting. The School of Commerce plays a major role in both the city and the region, offering part-time programs as far afield as Cape Breton and seeking out working professionals in Halifax through a flexible part-time MBA. Since 1990 it's had the only Executive MBA in Atlantic Canada and in 1999 will likely have the first and only PhD in the region.

The MBA would like to have greater national and international presence, says Paul Dixon, dean of the faculty. "But we're a community-based institution." So the school of business will probably remain a big fish in a small pond, though some students wish otherwise. "The biggest drawback," says one student, "is that for the quality, it doesn't have the profile it should in Central Canada. The quality is there." The fact is that Dalhousie's name is still far more recognizable once you leave the Maritimes.

In fall 1998 commerce moved into a brand-new $20-million facility ($1 million was provided by the province). SMU's modern campus fits neatly into a block in downtown Halifax. Its not-as-nice rivals in the Maritimes sometimes call it Robie Street High. Almost everything on campus is wheelchair accessible, which gives the campus a wide-open feel. The football field is near the centre of the campus, in pride of place.

MBA

Getting In

For entry in September 1998 the MBA received 260 applications and accepted 160 of those. The cut-off grad for admission is 3.0 out of 4.0, and the average grade of admitted students is 3.3. One recent change in the program is that students with a B.Comm and an average of at least B+ will be able to go directly into second year. The program does admit students without work experience.

Atmospherics

Though the undergrad program is fairly local, students come from all over the Maritimes for the MBA. The program also manages to draw a fair number of international students, particularly from China and India. But it still has the homey feel of the other programs. "It's very relaxed, more so than I thought it would be," says one student. "It's very co-operative as opposed to competitive. Everyone is in this together," adds another. Almost half the students in the MBA study part time, and the school does a good job of catering to these students.

Profs, Programs, and Particulars

SMU's MBA program has seen lots of small changes over the past few years. A recent emphasis is on the integration of different business fields. Students must now take a four-month business simulation course at the beginning of first year and another four-month one at the very end of their MBA career. In between, students must take a contemporary issues course and a business tools course. At the end of first year, there is a case competition that requires students to draw on what they have learned in all their classes. "I learned more just doing that case competition than in any course," says an alum.

The second thrust of the revision is to provide students with optional interdisciplinary specializations in second year. There are now packages of five courses in small business and entrepreneurship, human resources management, fiscal studies, and international development management. The faculty is hoping to place students from this last concentration in international placements during the summer of first year. In terms of functional areas, students say that finance and human resources are strong.

There is a major research project that requires students to get out into the community. "You can't get out of the program without doing field research," says Summers. "It's a PhD thesis on a small level," says one student. "My adviser used to spend nights with me in the computer lab. I don't think that would happen in a big school." There are also other opportunities for field research, particularly through the Atlantic Canada Opportunities Agency (ACOA), which links students up with companies interested in exporting to the Eastern US. Students help mainly with market research. Saint Mary's Business Development Centre is another source for interesting projects.

Living It Up

Students hang out in the MBA lounge and Tim Hortons in the MBA building. "Recreation is definitely a big part of the program," says one MBA. There are no MBA classes held on Friday, so Thursday nights at the Gorsebrook are packed with MBAs. Off-campus pubs include the Sea Horse and My Father's Moustache. Many students are involved in intramural sporting activities, particularly baseball and softball. (The quarterback of the football team is an MBA student.) A number of students participate in a 24-hour Labatt relay race that raises money for charity.

The MBA Society is the only club for MBA students, but the Commerce Society, ACE, AIESEC, and the Accounting Society are open to MBAs as well as to commerce students.

The Payoff

After years of being left to their own devices for their job search, MBAs now have an MBA placement office within the business school. The staff of the new office is working to attract more recruiters to SMU and is busy setting up job-search workshops. The school managed to survey all the members of the class of '97 and found that 85% were employed at graduation. Average salary was about $43,500.

Executive MBA

When the EMBA was first founded in 1990, there was some doubt in the institution about whether it would work. Would Maritimers be willing to fork over massive amounts of cash for an executive program? "It turned out to be much more popular than we expected," says Hermann Schwind, director of the program.

The EMBA takes in middle and senior managers from across Atlantic Canada, anyone from the self-employed to the CEO of a company with 200 employees. There is a small contingent of students from government and the armed forces. The program will accept people who don't have an undergrad degree. Since 1996 all students must have access to a computer and modem. A handful of managers from the Chinese company Min Metals have also participated in the EMBA.

Classes are every two weeks, Friday and Saturday. People fly in from as far away as Charlottetown, Saint John, St. John's, and Sydney. Class is held on the eighth floor of the World Trade Centre in Halifax. "It was more like going to a nice office building than a university classroom," says an alumni. Fancy candle-lit meals are served to students in the World Trade Centre.

The program starts with workshops that bring people up to speed in accounting, computers, math, and stats. Most courses are required but there is the choice of three electives. In the past, these have focused on areas like international marketing or industrial relations. Students may do a research project. The EMBA also has a strong international component. There is an optional international trip that sends about 15 students on a two-week trip to Hong Kong, China, and Malaysia. The most recent change in the program is that computers are now fully integrated.

There's an extraordinary sense of community even among EMBA students. Upon graduation, the entire class of 1996 formed its own company, Masters Group Ventures Ltd., because participants wanted more contact than a mere annual reunion. Part of the company's mission? Lending a hand to floundering companies and finding new managers for them.

The Bottom Line

A-list Alumni

William Dwight Roberts MBA '76: Secretary General, North American National Broadcasters Association (NANBA)

Gradventures

TecKnowledge Healthcare Systems Inc. (Dorothy Spence MBA '95 and Linda Weaver MBA '94)

Foreign Affairs

The business school has several exchanges with universities abroad, four of which are actually used—in Mexico, the US, Norway, and England. All students at Saint Mary's can go on exchange to universities in China, Vietnam, and Japan. The university also has a trilateral linkage through NAFTA, which sends students to study in the US and Mexico.

Money for Nothing

MBAs are eligible for nine named awards that are worth between $200 and $2,200, and 20 graduate awards worth $2,000 to $5,000. Eighteen students work as TAs at a salary of about $380 per semester.

Contacts

The Frank H. Sobey Faculty of Commerce • Saint Mary's University • Halifax, NS • B3H 3C3 • (902) 420-5422 • www.stmarys.ca/academic/commerce

SAINT MARY'S UNIVERSITY—VITAL STATISTICS

total university enrollment	7,251
total full-time undergrad enrollment	4,923
number of full-time professors in the faculty of commerce	63
number of part-time professors	82
number of women professors	13 full-time; 22 part-time

MBA

full-time enrollment	167
part-time enrollment	124
size of entering class	N/A
women students	37%
out-of-province students	12%
international students	17%
students straight from undergrad	N/A
average age	32
tuition	$750 per course
tuition for international students	$1,380 per course
length of program	2 years; 1 year for business grads
number of applications to the program	260
number of offers made	160
cut-off grade for admission	3.0 out of 4.0
average grade of admittees	3.3
average GMAT	561
years of work experience required	none
average years of work experience	5.5 years

size of core classes	28
size of electives	13
classes taught by full-time faculty	88%
grads employed at graduation	85%
number of recruiters	N/A
grads hired through placement office	N/A
average base starting salary	$43,500
what employment figures are based on	100% of the class of '97

Executive MBA

enrollment	45
women students	33%
average age	40
average GMAT	575
years of work experience required	5
average years of work experience	17
cost of program	$27,000

University of Saskatchewan

Unlike its neighbour in Manitoba, the University of Saskatchewan's College of Commerce is content to remain a regional business school. The university's motto is "God and Country" (*Deo et Patriae*), but it might as well read "For God, for country, and for Saskatchewan." As the province's flagship university, founded in 1907, the institution feels a responsibility to provide lots of programs to keep students in the province.

The MBA is a small generalist program that draws a lot of part-time students from Saskatoon. Several courses have a focus on the Pacific Rim, which isn't quite as bizarre as it sounds, since the province does a lot of exporting to countries in that region. MBAs are an easy-going lot. Where would they go if proximity weren't an issue? "Wharton because it's No. 1 or maybe Western," says one, laughing. "But from what I've heard, I don't think MBA programs are all that different from each other."

> In 1995, the college started a pilot program for a First Nations MBA in a joint venture with Saskatchewan Indian Federated College—another instance of the university serving its constituents. "Right now bands are screaming for people with business education," says Jack Vicq, associate dean. This program has since been rolled into the regular MBA, and students who take a minimum of four courses in Aboriginal management receive an MBA with a concentration in Aboriginal studies.

The U of S has one of the few collegiate Gothic campuses in Western Canada. It's a very attractive campus with tree-lined paths and lots of greenery. The College of Commerce is in one of the more recent buildings. A new wing for the building with brand new case rooms is in the planning stages.

MBA

Getting In

Most recently the MBA program received 170 applications of which it accepted 105. Applicants need a minimum average of 70%; the average of admitted students was 78%. Students aren't required to have any work experience, but there is a large part-time contingent, and the average work experience is eight years.

Atmospherics

Unlike the commerce program, the MBA has good representation of international students (about 20%) and a small proportion of out-of-province students (5%). In fact, many students say that one of the strengths of the program is the good mix of people: younger people with less work experience, older part-timers, and international students. "We have a lot of part-time students who enrich the experience. We have people from so many industries," says an alum.

Students say that one of the best things about the program is the close interaction with professors. "You can learn a lot from them. They come from all kinds of backgrounds," says one student.

Profs, Programs, and Particulars

Saskatchewan's MBA is a generalist program. The basic MBA requires 20 courses of which six are electives. Students may complete a thesis, in which case they have three fewer electives. Those who forgo the thesis must do a research project, usually a consultancy project or a feasibility study.

> Course selection isn't huge, but there is the opportunity to do close work with a faculty member through a business research course. For instance, "there are pockets of internationalism at the faculty and if you seek them out, you can fashion a concentration," says a student. The program has a number of international activities that take place during the summer. One group of students goes to the Ukraine and does applied research for Western Canadian companies. The faculty also sends two groups to Japan.

This probably isn't the program for someone who already has a business degree. One student with a B.Comm commented, "I'm finding it too general. There isn't a lot of focus and it's repetitive." But students without that background are well satisfied with the program. "It's been extremely useful. Before I couldn't have put together a marketing plan and felt confident that the bank would accept it. The program is money well spent," says a student.

Living It Up

MBAs frequent a handful of pubs regularly, such as Alexander's, Cheers, and The Pat. Another student hangout is Mykonos, a Greek restaurant in the city. As well, there's the grad carrel room in the commerce building and Louis', the campus pub. The MBA Society organizes social events like pub nights and potluck dinners, sponsors student attendance at conferences, and brings in speakers from the community.

The Payoff

MBA placement is subsumed under the general placement office. The office is geared more toward undergrads than MBAs, but the help is quite good, say students. Unfortunately, says one, "the reputation of U of S affects recruiters. You don't get major recruiters from Calgary or Vancouver." Ninety percent of MBAs responding to college surveys had found permanent employment within six months. (The rate of response is not known.) About 20 firms come on campus to recruit MBAs and 40% of students found jobs through on-campus recruiting. Full-time students tend to find jobs in financial organizations, health care, and consulting firms. A number of people go on to marketing positions, either brand management or international marketing for emerging firms in biotechnology or computer software.

The Bottom Line

A-list Alumni

David Taylor MBA '83: President and CEO, Pacific & Western Credit Corp., London, ON

Gradventures

Trimension Training Consulting Group (Larry Goodfellow MBA '76)

What the Judges Think

1994 Canadian Chamber of Commerce in Hong Kong annual paper competition: 1st place

Foreign Affairs

The college of commerce has an agreement with a consortium of universities in Mexico.

Money for Nothing

Funding is sparse at the MBA level. Three or four students receive graduate scholarships worth $7,500. In addition, there are four graduate teaching fellowships of the same value. A few students are employed as graders on an hourly basis.

Other Options

- Master of science in accounting
- Master of professional accounting

Contacts

College of Commerce • University of Saskatchewan • 25 Campus Drive • Saskatoon, SK • S7N 5A7 • (306) 966-4785 • www.commerce.usask.ca

UNIVERSITY OF SASKATCHEWAN—VITAL STATISTICS

total university enrollment	17,370
total full-time undergrad enrollment	N/A
number of full-time professors in the college of commerce	53
number of part-time professors	N/A
number of women professors	12

MBA

full-time enrollment	46
part-time enrollment	79
size of entering class	55 full-time and part-time
women students	30%
out-of-province students	5%
international students	20%
students straight from undergrad	15%
average age	30
annual tuition	$3,570
annual tuition for international students	same
length of program	2 years
number of applications	170
number of acceptances	105
cut-off grade for admission	70%
average grade of admittees	78%
average GMAT	560
years of work experience required	none
average years of work experience	8 years

size of core classes	20 to 40
size of electives	10 to 35
classes taught by full-time faculty	96%
grads employed within six months of graduation	90%
number of on-campus recruiters	20
grads hired through placement office	40%
average starting salary	N/A
what employment figures are based on	N/A

Université de Sherbrooke

Ask your random Quebecer about Quebec's French-language MBA schools and you're likely to get the following classification: the École des Hautes Études Commerciales (HEC) is prestigious and a bit overbearing; Laval is large and a bit less prestigious; the Université du Québec à Montréal (UQAM) is young and considers itself more innovative than either; but l'Université de Sherbrooke is practical and less monstrous in size than the other three.

> Sherbrooke's Faculté d'administration has made its name with excellent co-op programs—the first in French Canada—and rigorous use of group work. In fact, it's probably the only MBA program that students say they chose in part for all the group work. Co-op is mandatory in the MBA. Sherbrooke has also begun stretching its tentacles toward Montreal. In 1989 it started an Executive MBA in the suburb of Longueuil; its main competition is Concordia's MBA.

Bilingualism is less common at Sherbrooke than it is at the other three French-language MBA schools, but most of the readings at the MBA level are still in English. The faculty tries to hunt down French copies for students who have trouble reading the language.

The university is a 15-minute bus ride from downtown Sherbrooke. The campus is peaceful and green, and on a clear day you can see Mount Orford. In 1997 the faculty moved into a brand new building.

MBA

Getting In

The MBA receives some 75 applications a year and accepts about 35. There is no automatic cut-off for grades. Students must have at least two years of work experience. "The idea of teamwork loses its meaning when the participants don't have any experience," says Serge Goudreau, assistant to the MBA director. Once the applicants' written material has passed muster, students go through a personal interview to confirm that they are right for the class. There is also a small part-time MBA that doesn't include co-op.

Atmospherics

With only 20 students a year, the atmosphere is friendly and cohesive. "Everybody knows everybody. You really have a good spirit," says one student. Relationships with profs, especially the younger ones, are good. Most are on a first-name basis with students.

Students spend all of first term in groups that have been chosen by the administrators to ensure they are as heterogeneous as possible. "You learn to work with people like you would in the job market. You get all the little problems that you'd get at work: people who work at the last minute; people who prepare in advance," says a student. A consultant trained in psychology works with dysfunctional groups to help sort them out.

Profs, Programs, and Particulars

The MBA at Sherbrooke is a generalist program that considers its strengths to be co-op and group work. A new shorter program started in September 1996. The program is now completed in four terms, or about one and a half years. There are three academic terms and one work term. Students can choose a course-only option or courses with a mini-thesis. Students in the part-time program complete everything but the work terms. There are no formal specializations.

A-list Alumni

- Pierre Perron MBA '79: President, Au Grain de Café Mont Tremblant Inc.
- Jean-Pierre Deschênes MBA '72: CEO, Coopérative Fédérée de Québec
- Paulin Tardif MBA '68: Chairman of the Board and CEO, Bestar Inc.

The teaching of the core has also undergone a change. Everything is now taught in an integrated fashion. There's a business simulation that everyone goes through. "We all felt that it was a great experience. You really get the feeling of having a business to manage. You have to think of the different parts," says a student.

Teaching is good, especially from the few part-time teachers. "The profs don't really have any choice about keeping up to date because students keep themselves up to date," says another student. Almost all marks are given for the group as a whole. The rare exams are the only occasions on which students are marked for individual work.

A universal complaint concerns limited course selection. With budget cuts, the number of electives has been reduced. Students would like more courses in their particular areas of interest. Courses with too few people enrolled end up not being offered. "Because we're a class of 20, we're only about three people per specialization," says a student. "It's harder to make the balance tip toward the courses you want." But group work has its uses: the class gets together and talks it out so that everyone gets some of the classes they want.

Co-op

Co-op has been mandatory since the MBA began. In the new program, there is only one work term, compared with two previously. It takes place during the summer after students have had two academic terms. The placement rate is 100% and the average salary is $545 a week. Most jobs are in Montreal and, to a lesser degree, Ottawa. Jobs are broad-based — it really depends on the student's interest.

Living It Up

Every Thursday there is a *cinq à sept* (five to seven) in le Sofa with the undergrads (which also stretches to *quatre à sept* and even *quatre à huit*). The MBAs also have their own little lounge upstairs with a fridge. The main hangout is Le Bahut, the campus pub. Two popular Sherbrooke pubs are Le café du palais and Le BlaBla.

Because the group is so small, the MBA Society is an informal gathering of people. The president of the Society sits on a faculty committee that looks at the direction of the programs. Parties are held in his apartment. There's a team of students that participates in the MBA Games. The REMDUS is the graduate students' association of the university.

The Payoff

The Service de Placement received 474 job postings for all programs in the faculty. The office keeps track of about 95% of the graduating class. Of those who graduated in August, 80% were employed by the following April. The average starting salary is $41,143.

Executive MBA

In many ways, the Executive MBA is part and parcel of the regular MBA. The group of students is small and there is a strong emphasis on group work.

The greatest concentration of participants comes from the greater Montreal area, but the program draws from as far away as the Gaspé, Quebec City, and Drummondville. Students range in age from 29 to 61. Classes are held once a week on alternating Fridays and Saturdays in the Complexe Saint Charles, an office building in Longueuil that the program rents.

The EMBA is unique in taking participants' academic background into account. Applicants with an undergraduate degree in business and lots of experience can forgo the first part of the program, which lasts 37 weeks. Students without that background must complete both halves of the program. Part two consists of five four-month sessions.

All teams except those in the final semester are chosen by administrators. There are a couple of intensive weekend sessions where participants practise their teamwork with the help of psychologists.

The Bottom Line

Foreign Affairs

The faculty has exchanges with 30 universities in Morocco, Burkina Faso, Tunisia, Germany, Ecuador, Argentina, Chile, Columbia, Guatemala, Costa Rica, Brazil, England, Spain, the US, France, and Sweden, and with Wilfrid Laurier and Simon Fraser in Canada.

Money for Nothing

There are 39 scholarships available to all students enrolled in the faculty of administration. The average value is $1,500. In addition MBAs can apply for four scholarships, two of them worth $1,000 and two worth $1,500. At present, there are no entering scholarships, but these should be available in 1998.

Other Options

- Master of Arts in Cooperative Development
- Master of Science in Administration
- Master of Taxation

Contacts

Faculté d'administration • Université de Sherbrooke • Sherbrooke, PQ • J1K 2R1 • (819) 821-7300 • www.usherb.ca/ADM/pp.htm

UNIVERSITÉ DE SHERBROOKE—VITAL STATISTICS

total university enrollment	22,000
number of full-time professors in the faculty of administration	54
number of part-time professors	40
number of women professors	7

MBA

full-time enrollment	40
part-time enrollment	25
size of entering class	35
women students	25%
out-of-province students	5%
international students	negligible
students straight from undergrad	none
average age	32
total tuition for Quebec students	$2,892
total tuition for Canadian students	$4,972
total tuition for international students	$14,332
length of program	16 months
number of applications	75
number of acceptances	35
cut-off grade for admission	N/A
average grade of admittees	N/A
average GMAT	not required
years of work experience required	2
average years of work experience	5

size of core classes	35
size of electives	15
classes taught by full-time faculty	75%
grads employed within eight months of graduation	80%
number of postings	474 for all programs in the faculty
grads hired through placement office	N/A
average starting salary	$41,143
what employment figures are based on	95% of the graduating class

Executive MBA

enrollment	100 to 110
women students	25%
average age	38
average GMAT	not required
years of work experience required	5
average years of work experience	12
cost of program	$19,000

Simon Fraser University

When the first people in the Executive MBA program made their way up Burnaby Mountain to Simon Fraser University over 30 years ago, they found student picketers at the top protesting their presence. In fact, the very idea of suits coming to this radical British Columbia campus, the Shangri-La of Canadian universities, was amusing.

Today business is one of the most popular majors at SFU. The Executive MBA is the faculty's flagship program and the only one in BC. The regular MBA has catered to a niche market far longer than many other programs. And the university was ranked first in its category in the 1997 *Maclean*'s survey. Meanwhile, the ideals of the academic quadrangle where students from all disciplines would meet, mingle, and become well-rounded humanists—one of the cherished principles on which the university was founded—have gone the way of the picketers.

Two other principles are intact, however: accessibility to education and flexibility. (One could argue that accepting those executives back in 1968 was merely a fulfillment of the university's mandate of providing courses to people who might not get them otherwise.) Simon Fraser continues to offer some of the most flexible programs around. It is one of a handful of universities that runs on the trimester system, which allows MBA students to take classes throughout the year.

Having first brought the executives to the mountain, the university moved to bring the mountain to the executives in 1989. Simon Fraser's campus, at Harbour Centre, in downtown Vancouver, opened in a sleek office building. Most MBA courses continue to be offered on the Burnaby campus. Arthur Erickson's concrete acropolis, the physical quadrangle, is still the main structure though a couple of new buildings have sprouted since the opening of the university in 1965. The view from any campus window is breathtaking: "I'm looking at the ocean, snow on the mountain, sailboats on the water," a student says.

MBA

Getting In

SFU has introduced a new specialized MBA program in 1999 in Financial Services, with another specialized program in management technology to start in 2000. Depending on the success of these programs, there is a chance that the regular MBA program may be abandoned. For now SFU has virtually abolished the first year of the regular MBA which means that students must come in with an undergraduate degree in business. They then complete the MBA in one year.

For September 1998 the faculty received 298 applications of which it accepted 51. Students must have a minimum GPA of 3.0, and the average GPA of admitted students is 3.3. Work experience is neither required nor preferred, and three-quarters of students enter the program straight from undergrad. Of those with work experience, the average is two years.

Atmospherics

When first year still existed some students complained that it was very competitive, perhaps owing to the large number of students fresh from their undergraduate degree. "I was expecting a very diverse group of people, and it wasn't what I got," one student says. "In my year, I'm one of the oldest and I'm only 24." One grad speculates that for students without work experience in the Vancouver area, SFU is the program of choice; students who come from other provinces are more likely to have the work experience.

"There is a really great relationship between profs and students," a student says. "All are on a first-name basis." All students must complete a substantial project in the program, and many become close to their faculty adviser.

Profs, Programs, and Particulars

Simon Fraser's MBA is a cross between an MSc and an MBA. "Our emphasis is on training staff specialists rather than line workers," says Stan Shapiro, former dean of the faculty. Part of the rationale for accepting students without work experience comes from this focus. If a student were already a financial analyst, the reasoning goes, there wouldn't be a lot of training the MBA could provide.

> A major complaint of students with work experience is the huge number of classmates without experience. "They say, 'Oh yeah, we're turning out specialists.' But all the students know is theory. What's the good of being a specialist if no one will hire you because you don't have the experience?" one grad remarks.

Despite this caveat, the program does a good job of training specialists. "It's wonderful preparation for a PhD," says an alum. Quality of teaching is high. Concentrations are available in accounting, finance, human resources management, international business, management science and information systems, marketing, and policy analysis. Policy, HR, international business, and MIS are strong. Students are encouraged to take courses in other faculties.

The depth of specialization comes not so much from the second-year courses as from the major project that everyone must complete. An accounting student might do a study on environmental auditing. One student with an MA in theology, worked on a leadership program, bringing in issues of ethics and spirituality. Students have the choice of writing a thesis that is worth three courses or a research project that is worth one. The research project tends to be more applied than the thesis and it doesn't have a defence.

Given the research orientation, this is a fairly theoretical program. But there are opportunities for more applied research. Businesses will post project opportunities, back-burner ideas, and so forth, through the Project Clearinghouse, a computer database that students have access to. It's up to students to create a more applied program for themselves. While the dominant style of instruction is the lecture, a small group of professors teach primarily through case studies. MBA students can take the odd course from the EMBA, though you can't make a habit of it—EMBA students pay big bucks for their program, after all.

> **Co-op**
>
> In September 1996, the MBA inaugurated the start of its co-op program. Seven students were enrolled as of October. There are two required work terms and a third optional one. Students may enter the program after having completed two senior-level courses or all of the first-year courses. Some postings are strictly for MBA students, but a number of positions are cross-listed with the commerce program. A word of caution: "Many of the students who don't have work experience will find it very difficult to compete with senior undergraduates," says the co-op coordinator.

Living It Up

Intramural sports are very popular in the MBA. Hockey, volleyball, and baseball are all strong. Students hang out in the MBA lounge, at the Highland Pub, and at the Mountain Shadow, the pub at the bottom of the hill. People have also been known to camp out in the computer office for 24 hours at a time.

The MBA association was started three years ago and acts principally as a resource for students. Some students are involved in Students for Responsible Business, a group which gets students involved in community activism.

The Payoff

The focus of career services used to be "teaching people to fish, rather than throwing them a fish," as the former dean of the faculty used to say. Many students, however, would have preferred a fish. But since 1998 MBA students have had access to a new placement centre within the faculty with a full-time placement officer. Part of this person's job is to bring more recruiters on campus. For the time being, there are no statistics on grads employed within six months of graduation or starting salaries.

> **A-list Alumni**
>
> - Harold William Buddle MBA '87: CEO, Capital City Savings and Credit Union Ltd.
> - Carollyne Conlinn MBA '86: Vice-President, Business Development, Versa Services Ltd.
> - William P. Dover MBA '79: President, W.P. Dover & Associates
> - Clifford Hinton MBA '76: President and CEO, TransTech Interactive Training Inc.
> - Sandy Michael Fulton MBA '75: President and CEO, Pacific Forest Products Ltd.

MBA in Financial Services

The new MBA in Financial Services started in January 1999 with a cohort of 50. The program is a joint venture between the business schools of SFU and the University of British Columbia, the most substantial cooperation between the two schools thus far. The program, which is entirely part-time, targets those employed in financial institutions such as banks, insurance companies, and credit unions, though students need not be employed in the sector to apply to the program. A consortium of 12 or so companies are involved in the MBA: as an advisory body, for case study and research sites, and for employment opportunities. There are two streams: a management of financial services organizations stream and a certification stream, in which students take courses that will enable them to graduate with both an MBA and a designation from an organization such as the Institute of Canadian Bankers or the Society for Management Accountants. The program is provisionally priced at about $20,000.

Management of Technology MBA

The new MBA in the management of technology (MOT) will likely come on-line in January 2000. This program, which will also start with a cohort of 50, is a full-time program of nine months that targets people with scientific background, such as engineers and those who work in the computer industry. Students will need to have a recent business degree or (have completed Simon Fraser's new Graduate Diploma in Business Administration (GDBA). The GDBA courses will be available through the Internet. As in the MBA in Financial Services, a consortium of technology companies will work in partnership with SFU on the MOT.

Executive MBA

The University of Toronto likes to say that its EMBA, founded in the early 1980s, was the first in Canada, because Simon Fraser's started out offering evening rather than weekend courses and charging fees that were similar to the regular MBA. "It lacked all the aura that goes with the high-fee program," says Daniel Shapiro, director of the EMBA at SFU. But for all intents and purposes, SFU's was the first. From the beginning it focused on working professionals and coddled them in the manner of executive programs.

The EMBA now has both a weekend stream, all day Friday and Saturday every other week, and an evening stream, Wednesday and Thursday evening every week. It also charges the glamorous price of $22,000 for the night program and $28,000 for the weekend one. (The weekend stream includes accommodation and pricey meals.) The program unabashedly targets the middle manager. "And no matter what they say, most programs do," Shapiro says.

Students take nine required courses and two electives and prepare a substantial project. There is international content in every course and international business is always offered as an elective, but there are no international trips in the curriculum. The other electives vary from year to year; in 1996 some of the electives were managing innovation and managing negotiations and conflict. The program will sometimes bring in outside experts to teach the electives.

The project is the distinguishing feature of the EMBA. Students may choose between a strategic analysis, normally based on the student's own company, or a public policy analysis, which would most likely relate to the student's field. The project is supervised by a faculty member. One student, a member of the RCMP, wrote a paper about stock exchange regulations that was discussed in the BC Legislative Assembly. In scope, the project is thesis-like: it goes through many rewritings and is meant to be "an exercise in rigorous thought and analysis," Shapiro says.

The Bottom Line

What the Judges Think

- 1996 MBA Canada-Hong Kong Trade Competition: 1st place for a proposal to market BC ginseng in Asia
- 1996 MBA Canada-Hong Kong Trade Competition: 2nd place for a proposal to market water-conserving shower heads in Hong Kong
- 1996 MBA Canada-Hong Kong Trade Competition: 1st place in the Western category for a proposal to market Pacific micro-brewing companies

Money for Nothing

The MBA program awards about 35 scholarships worth $4,250 each. Simon Fraser also has an extremely generous teaching assistant package. About 50 MBA students work as teaching assistants for an annual salary of $4,500.

Options

Master in Resource Management

Contacts

Faculty of Business Administration • Simon Fraser University • 8888 University Drive • Burnaby, BC • V5A 1S6 • (604) 291-3708 • www.bus.sfu.ca

SIMON FRASER UNIVERSITY—VITAL STATISTICS

total university enrollment	23,200
total full-time undergrad enrollment	9,409
number of full-time professors in the school of business	48
number of part-time professors	23
number of women professors	12 full-time
MBA	
full-time enrollment	132
part-time enrollment	none
size of entering class	51
women students	40%
out-of-province students	N/A
international students	20%
students straight from undergrad	75%
average age	26
tuition	$800 per semester
tuition for international students	$2,400 per semester

length of program	20 months; 12 months for business grads
number of applications	298
number of acceptances	51
cut-off grade for admission	3.0 out of 4.0
average grade of admittees	3.3
average GMAT	610
years of work experience required	none
average years of work experience	2.5 to 3
size of core classes	30
size of electives	20
classes taught by full-time faculty	72%
grads employed within six months of graduation	no formal tracking

Executive MBA

enrollment	120
women students	25%
average age	37
average GMAT	600
years of work experience required	10
average years of work experience	12 to 15
cost of program	$22,000 for the night program $28,000 for the weekend program

University of Toronto

Times are good at the University of Toronto's Faculty of Management. Bob Prichard, the president of the university, has decided that with world-class schools of law and medicine, there's no reason why management should lag behind—hence a gentler budget cut. Joseph L. Rotman, alumnus and benefactor, has given the faculty $15 million to hire more world-class faculty members. (The gift, which is payable in installments, can also be withheld if the Rotman Foundation determines that the faculty is not living up to its own world-class aspirations.)

The most visible sign of this new well being is the faculty's gorgeous $24-million building, the Joseph L. Rotman Centre. The MBA facilities used to be in a grimy building with a Royal Bank branch in it, and freshmen about to open their first bank account would huddle in the faculty's lobby. In the new building, the flooring is from Germany, the limestone from Indiana, and there are Inuit sculptures and Robert Motherwell prints in some offices. A favourite piece of art is the black leather bustier and jacket daubed with the words "Killer Rabbit" that oscillates in a glass case in the lobby. (You know you're leaving the building late when even the bunny has been turned off.) "If you want to be a world-class business school, you have to have a world-class building," says an administrator.

But enough of the superficials. The Faculty of Management is one of the top business schools in Canada. It has more members of the Royal Society among its faculty than any other Canadian business school. Executive education—which includes non-degree programs, the Executive MBA, and mammoth custom programs that the faculty runs for companies such as Bell Canada—now generates about $5 million a year in revenue.

> These days, the faculty is trying awfully hard to persuade people it's not a quantitative school. "Twenty years ago the stereotype used to be, if you want a backroom analyst, go to Toronto, but if you want a general manager to run your company, go to Western," says Hugh Arnold, former dean of the faculty. "Sometimes we still get labelled as a quant jock program, but I don't think that's the case. We don't have people with green eye-shades poring over sheets of numbers." U of T still sends a substantial proportion of grads into finance jobs, but for the first time ever, consulting claimed the same percentage of 1998 grads as investment banking. Add to this the fact the school recently acquired a new dean, Roger Martin, who is a former vice-president of Monitor Corp., and it looks like U of T is remaking itself as more than just a finance enclave.

U of T's campus in downtown Toronto sprawls over several acres. The campus is a patchwork of smaller college campuses, many of them historic buildings around a green. There's the odd unhappy architectural experiment like U of T's Robarts Library (aka Fort Book) but for the most part the campus is very pleasing.

MBA

Getting In

The MBA received 960 applications for entry in September 1998, of which it accepted a classified number. Suffice it to say that the entering class has about 120 full-time students in it. Students need an undergraduate degree with a minimum grade of 3.0 in their final year. Four-year degrees are viewed more favourably than three-year ones. Students need a minimum of two years' work experience, but the program makes an exception for students in the MBA/LLB program, who may enter straight from undergrad.

Atmospherics

The full-time MBA is a close-knit program. "This is a very social program. You work hard and you play hard," says a second-year student. "You can't be too high-strung," says another. "You have to know how to relax and blow off steam."

> The program starts with a mandatory four-day orientation where students are hauled off to a resort north of Toronto. There are lots of team-building exercises and students are introduced to the teams they will be in all year. "When you walk into class, you know people already," says a student.

One student, who doesn't even wear green eye-shades, wishes the course were "more finance oriented." A former humanities student says the program is definitely easier with a quant background. But an engineer disagrees, saying, "I'd never had so much reading before."

There is another dimension to the faculty—an electronic one. The faculty has its own internal Bulletin Board System

(BBS), and every study group has an electronic folder on it. The system was designed by a former grad who has since set up his own business, Embanet Corp., providing business schools with a BBS system.

Gradventures
• Clairvest Group Inc. (Joseph L. Rotman MBA '60)
• Novopharm Ltd. (Leslie Dan MBA '59)
• Embanet Corp. (Jeffrey Feldberg MBA '95)

Profs, Programs, and Particulars

U of T's MBA is geared toward general management with the opportunity to take specialized classes in second year. First year is devoted to the core. As of the fall 1997, the first semester is divided into two seven-week halves with one week between them that teaches managerial skills and leadership. Second semester is broken up by a similar week that focuses on the international perspective. Prominent speakers are brought in for these one-week periods. Professors are starting to integrate the teaching of the core by using the same projects and cases across courses.

Second year is an entirely free year. But the program is moving toward providing some structure, such as sequencing of courses, for students who want to specialize. Some students say they'd like more diversity in course selection, particularly in the consulting area.

> The selection of finance courses is excellent and the city is an amazing resource. It's easy to cull guest lecturers from the Toronto business scene, and people on Bay Street are often auditing classes. "If we need a course in finance, we go down and ask the VP of Dominion," boasts Glen Whyte, executive director of the program. Some students also choose to take part-time jobs in brokerage firms. "The resources you have available at work are amazing," says an alumna.

Students say there's a good balance between practice and theory (i.e., lectures in first year, cases in second). "You've got to get up to speed to do a case. Having no business background, I wanted to learn a bit before I had to talk about it," says one student. Adds Whyte: "There's nothing so practical as a good theory. I think there's a false dichotomy between theory and practice."

In past years, the quality of teaching was a problem, but the faculty has cracked down on poor teachers, while rewarding good ones and establishing a mentoring program for other faculty to learn from them. "If you don't have a demonstrable ability to teach, even if your research is great, you won't be teaching in the MBA," says Whyte.

Living It Up

On Thirsty Thursdays, which are every Thursday, students go to assorted bars in the area, such as The Madison, The Duke of York, and The Bedford Ballroom. There's an MBA lounge in the Rotman Centre where students hang out between classes.

There are many more opportunities for involvement at the MBA level than at the commerce level. The Graduate Business Council represents MBA students at U of T. IMPACT is the student consulting group which used to advise small businesses and now has soared to corporate clients. ("The building makes a big impression. I think we get some of the contracts through the building," says one student.) There's an MBA yearbook and an MBA student magazine called *The Bloor Street Journal*. Other clubs are the Business & Technology Group, the Business Challenge Association, the Entrepreneur Association, the Finance Association, the International Business Association, the Marketing Association, and the Strategy Association. There is a student-organized MBA Business Conference and the Unilever Speaker Series, which brings high-profile speakers to campus.

The Payoff

The MBA Career Centre, which is located in the Rotman building, managed to reach 80% of 1998 grads and found that 94% were employed within three months of graduation. A total of 396 companies recruited the class of '98, of which 73 recruited on campus. In terms of functional area, finance jobs represented 43% of placements, consulting 29%, marketing 10%, business development 8%, operations 6%, and other areas 4%. In recent years, U of T has seen a large increase in the numbers of students entering the consulting industry. The class of '98 has the highest numbers yet, with investment banking and consulting industries each claiming 26% of the class (only 10% of the class of '96 accepted a consulting position). These consulting figures can only increase with the appointment of Martin to the deanship. After investment banking and consulting, corporate/commercial banking has the most grads with 22%, followed by consumer goods 11%, and high-tech 5%. The average starting salary was $78,400.

> **A-list Alumni**
>
> - Wendy Cukier MBA '86: Co-Founder of Canada's Coalition for Gun Control
> - John Cassaday MBA '81: President and CEO, CTV Television Network Ltd.
> - Peter Bacon MBA '81: President and CEO, Hongkong Bank Discount Trading Inc.
> - Ruth Armstrong MBA '81: President, Vision Management Services
> - Brian E. Hickey MBA '70: President and CEO, Harlequin Enterprises Ltd.

Executive MBA

U of T's EMBA, founded in 1983, is the second oldest in Canada. Most participants are managers in mid-career from Toronto's downtown core, where U of T competes with EMBAs from Queen's and Western, not to mention York's substantial executive programs. The program takes two years to complete. Classes are held in the Rotman Centre every week on alternating Fridays and Saturdays. There are two short residential periods in August of each year.

The EMBA teaches general management with a focus on globalization and strategic management. Classes are taught in an integrated fashion throughout. There are two international trips: a three-day visit to the US or Mexico in year one and a 10-day trip in year two where students go further afield. In January of 1997, second-year students went to Hong Kong and Shanghai.

> Because there is so much group work, the program has an individual rite of passage that also acts as quality control. Between years one and two, students must write a comprehensive exam, usually a large case study. They defend their analysis in front of faculty and two alumni, and if they fail, must take the exam again until they pass it. The program also has a required industry project that students begin working on in the summer between the two halves of the program.

As for weaknesses in the program? "Because it is very demanding we tend to have more of an emphasis on the hard skills like finance and marketing. We oftentimes don't do enough on the soft side, how to mentor, how to deal with people. But I think that's characteristic of MBA programs across Canada," says Joe D'Cruz, director of the program.

The Bottom Line

Foreign Affairs

There are 11 MBA exchanges with schools in Austria, France, Mexico, Singapore, and Hong Kong. Three more in Italy and Germany are in the planning stages.

Money for Nothing

All entering MBAs in the top 20% of the class receive a scholarship worth $3,600. There is an additional group of scholarships for second-years, ranging from $100 to $5,000. It is uncommon for MBAs to work as teaching assistants, but a few students do work as research assistants.

Options

- Joint MBA/LLB
- Master of management and professional accounting
- PhD

Contacts

Joseph L. Rotman Centre for Management • University of Toronto • 105 St. George St. • Toronto, ON • M5S 3E6 • (416) 978-5703 • www.mgmt.utoronto.ca

UNIVERSITY OF TORONTO—VITAL STATISTICS

total university enrollment	53,624
total full-time undergrad enrollment	30,859
number of full-time professors in the Faculty of Management	60
number of part-time professors	45
number of women professors	16 full-time
MBA	
full-time enrollment	240
part-time enrollment	190
size of entering class	120 full-time; 60 part-time
women students	38%
out-of-province students	N/A
international students	30%
students straight from undergrad	5%
average age	28

annual tuition and fees	$8,000
annual tuition and fees for international students	$14,000
length of program	2 years
number of applications	960
number of acceptances	N/A
cut-off grade for admission	3.0 in final year of undergrad
average grade of admittees	B+ to A-
average GMAT	660
years of work experience required	2
average years of work experience	4
size of core classes	60
size of electives	8 to 40
classes taught by full-time faculty	N/A
grads employed within six months of graduation	94%
number of on-campus recruiters	about 80
grads hired through placement office	56%
average base starting salary	$78,400
what employment figures are based on	80% of the class of '98

Executive MBA

enrollment	110
women students	23%
average age	38
average GMAT	570
years of work experience required	8
average years of work experience	13
cost of program	$49,000

University of Victoria

Do you have a pioneering streak? Do you shudder at the thought of being a number cruncher? Have you always had a secret suspicion that life might really be better on the West Coast? If you can say yes to any of these questions, the University of Victoria's faculty of business school may be the place for you.

When the embryonic business school began laying the foundation for an MBA program in 1988, the plan was to offer something quite traditional: two years in length, functional areas in first year and electives in second. But by the time the faculty was actually set up, the theories behind MBAs were starting to change and the original blueprint was abandoned.

The result was an MBA program that students described as "not a typical business program." The five pillars on which the program stand are multidisciplinarity, skills training, global perspectives, practicality/problem-solving, and innovation. The faculty does its best to keep these principles coursing through its program. "The program struck me at the time as being really different from all the others," says an MBA student from Ontario.

> But UVic's salad days are coming to a close. In 1998 new dean Roger Wolff, came out with a strategic plan for the faculty which characterized its current position as "a small unfocused business school [living] with the daily reality that [it] is overextended and underfunded." While the business school could remain a regional school, the decision has been made to refocus the school and give it more of an international orientation.

UVic started life in 1903 as an affiliate of McGill and acquired its university charter in 1963. Victoria is idyllic. "It's very delicate: there are lots of roses and rhododendrons and little old people," says an administrator. The air is balmy and the ocean is down the hill from the university. There's a fountain in the centre of campus with ducks swimming in it. The business school moved into a brand new building in the summer of 1997.

MBA

Getting In

The MBA program accepts only a very small number of applicants each year. It receives 250 applications yearly and sends out 70 to 80 acceptances. Ali Dastmalchian, former director of the program, says, "I find myself advising a whole host of applicants to go elsewhere, especially people who want to specialize in a functional area." He recommends the program to students who don't have a business degree or who've been out of a business program for at least seven years. You'll need an overall average of B to be admitted to the program. Work experience is strongly preferred but isn't an absolute requirement.

Atmospherics

The MBA program is small and there is excellent rapport between the students. The camaraderie starts right from the beginning during orientation when students are whisked away to a nearby resort for a few days. "I thought it was great, because we really got to know each other before classes started," says one student. "During the term you're too stressed out to get to know people."

Because the program is still pretty new, students have a lot of impact on it. "I was very impressed by how fast they changed things if we didn't like them," recalls an alumna. "Students have grown to be far more proactive and entrepreneurial. They're buying into this model. They don't wait for something to go wrong and then complain," says Dastmalchian.

But the rapid pace of the program can be tiring. "They told us at the beginning, 'Forget the fact that you have a life,'" says one student, admitting that she had never been so stressed out.

Profs, Programs, and Particulars

The program consists of four modules, a corporate internship, and a major project. The first module is a one-month preparation module that brings students up to speed on negotiation and presentation skills, and basics in math, statistics, and software. The second and third modules, lasting four months each, are each made up of six six-week courses. Some topics like accounting and finance are taught over 12 weeks. These two modules introduce the basic building blocks of business and bring in more advanced material, such as corporate law, international business, and consulting methods.

Each module is broken up by two industry projects that the entire class works on, in teams of five or six. The first might involve a study of financial institutions in Victoria and require students to come up with financial statements and economic forecasts. But the last project might concentrate on something as large as the BC arts and film industry and the strategic issues it faces. By the time all four projects are done, "you leave the course in April and everything clicks together. You see it from a different perspective," says a student.

The fourth module is the specialization module. MBA students have the same choice in specialization as the commerce students: entrepreneurship, tourism management or international business. Students must also complete a major project, which may be a traditional thesis or a consulting project. About 70% of students choose the consulting project.

> There is also an optional executive mentor program that, so far, all students have participated in. Mentors, most of them senior Victoria business people, even attend part of orientation to play golf with the students.

Before starting on the corporate internship, students have the opportunity to go on the MBA Study Tour in Southeast Asia, which takes place in Singapore, Malaysia, and Hong Kong. Students spend five weeks studying at the University of Malaya in Kuala Lumpur or the Chinese University of Hong Kong. They also work on projects in Southeast Asian companies and some students stay on for internships in these companies.

Students like the innovation in the program, though some still hanker after traditional specializations such as marketing or finance. But the bottom line is "Victoria is not going to be known as a number-crunching school. We're going to be seen as people who come out of the program and will start up our own business or bring an entrepreneurial flair to an existing organization," says one student.

> **Internship**
>
> The internship requirement is flexible. If you have several years of work experience the faculty waives the requirement, but if you have no experience, you'll have to do two work terms. Though everyone eventually does find a job, the process can be difficult because of the school's location. The co-op office helps with jobs but students need to do their own job-hunting as well. Some go through their corporate mentor and others start their own small business with the same wage subsidy as the undergrads.

Living It Up

The MBA society organizes one or two social events a month. MBA students also go to the Commerce banquet. "We profit from what the undergrads do," says an MBA student. There are several neighbourhood pubs that are popular with MBA students, including Swans, Hunters, and The Drawing Room. Nearby Camosun College has a training school for chefs with a small restaurant, and some MBAs go there for lunch.

The Payoff

Recruiting is done mostly by corporate internship employers. One alumnus managed to parlay the mentor program into a permanent job as a human resources consultant in his mentor's company. The Career Opportunities Adviser netted 264 postings in 1996, some of them for more than one position. UVic's first MBAs graduated in 1994, and there are no statistics on average salaries or percentage employed within six months of graduation.

The Bottom Line

Foreign Affairs

The faculty of business has exchanges with universities in Japan, Taiwan, Korea, Thailand, Hong Kong, Indonesia, Germany, Mexico, Singapore, Malaysia, and France.

Money for Nothing

There are five scholarships available to MBA students, ranging in value from $1,000 to $11,000. The faculty also hires five to 10 research assistants yearly and pays them $14.99 an hour.

Contacts

Faculty of Business • University of Victoria • PO Box 3015 • Victoria, BC • V8W 3P1 • (250) 721-8264 • www.business.uvic.ca

UNIVERSITY OF VICTORIA—VITAL STATISTICS	
total university enrollment	17,145
undergrad enrollment	15,327
number of full-time professors in the school of business	27
number of part-time professors	about 20
number of women professors	5
MBA	
full-time enrollment	84
size of entering class	46
women students	33%
out-of-province students	70%

international students	25%
students straight from undergrad	8%
average age	28 to 30
total tuition	$8,000
total tuition for international students	same
length of program	18 months
number of applications	250
number of acceptances	70 to 80
cut-off grade for admission	B
average grade of admittees	B+ to A-
average GMAT	600
years of work experience required	none
average years of work experience	7
size of core classes	46
size of electives	12
classes taught by full-time faculty	70%
grads employed within six months of graduation	no formal tracking

University of Western Ontario

The only reason anyone gives for choosing to attend the University of Western Ontario's business school is, "I wanted to go to the best business school in Canada." This would be insufferable if there weren't some truth to the claim.

So what does "the best" mean? First: great faculty members. Many profs consult for major Canadian corporations. What's more, students are assured access to their profs because all faculty are full time. Second: excellent job prospects. "An alumna told me that if she stands on a corner of Bay Street for half an hour, she'll see 15 of her classmates walk by," says an alumna. Third: a long tradition, which means eager recruiters, droves of high-profile alumni as potential contacts, and impressive resources. Fourth: a belief in teaching. And finally, there's the fact that all the palaver about "best this, best that" becomes self-perpetuating: people say it's the best, so the best want to go there, and so on.

> In 1995 the business school received $11 million from the Richard M. Ivey family and foundation and renamed itself the Richard Ivey School of Business, in honour of the 1972 alumnus. Ivey is an appropriate name. The business school was modelled after Harvard's business school and for many years Ivey faculty came from that ivy league institution. Ivey inherited the case-study method from Harvard and now produces more case studies than anyone in the world besides Harvard. All programs at Ivey employ the method, which gives the place a corporate identity unlike any other Canadian business school.

After you've slogged through more than 600 cases, you too will no doubt maintain that there is no other way to learn the craft of business. Says Jeffrey Gandz, dean of academic programs: "I like to tell students, 'In the last 20 minutes you've just developed a theory that it took Michael Porter seven years to develop.' When you lecture, it's one size fits all, but in the case-study method you're going through a series of individual development moves." The method teaches good communication skills, since students must constantly defend their point of view in front of their peers. "People plan. They say 'I'm going to speak in class today and this is what I'm going to say,'" says a student. Picture a roomful of Type-As all competing for airtime and all being marked on participation.

But perhaps because Ivey has always been "the best," it hasn't always been the first. Queen's was the first to offer a videoconferencing Executive MBA in 1994, followed by Ivey a year later. Queen's was also one of the first business schools to privatize its program. In the spring of 1997, Ivey announced that it would follow that move, a decision that will eventually see tuition rise to $36,000. And in some ways, the school sounds almost conservative. No talk, for instance, of making the regular two-year MBA any shorter.

In 1998 Western made its business school wireless. Students now have access to the Internet and e-mail through their laptops without ever having to plug in to a phone jack—a welcome addition, since all entering MBA students must own their own notebook computer.

The 72 buildings on Western's 1878 campus don't actually have ivy on them, but most of them are still respectably collegiate gothic. The campus is huge—there are even a couple of traffic lights along the main drag—but students get around mostly on the many foot paths. The suburban leafiness and six-lane streets of London lie just beyond the university gates.

MBA

Getting In

The MBA program received 936 applications for the entering class of 1998 and accepted 300. Aside from what Gandz calls "basic brightness" as measured by the GMAT and grades, the school of business looks for a student body that's diverse in background, culture, experience, and, preferably, gender. The business school requires students to have at least two years of work experience. Involvement in outside activities and evidence of leadership are important as well. Students need minimum grades of 70%, and the average of admitted students is 78%.

A few students who have graduated from the undergrad business program are admitted directly into the second year of the MBA, provided they have the requisite work experience. Western also accepts some students who don't have an undergrad degree if they have a professional designation or extensive work experience.

Atmospherics

During the first year of the program students are divided into three sections of 65 students. They take all their first-year classes with this group and work with them in assigned teams and study groups. Each section has acquired its reputation: Section 1, "studious, antisocial, quiet," explains one student;

Section 3, "rowdy, outgoing, very party;" and Section 2, somewhere between the two, "serious but fun-loving." It's a reputation that maintains itself from year to year even with a different batch of students.

While students are competitive, classroom atmosphere is comradely. "Everyone is meant to get through it together," says a student. Besides, says another, "Everyone is so different. It's not like a dentistry class with five people and only two of them will have teeth to pull." During first-year classes, the student from each section who makes the silliest/funniest/most self-evident comment of the week is awarded a rubber chicken. The recipient keeps a transcript of all funny comments during the following week and each section votes on the next chicken.

The MBA association runs a weeklong orientation for new students that has 90% attendance. "It's very important to make friends in this program. Sometimes you're juggling nine cases. You're getting used to 12- and 13-hour days," advises an alum.

The MBA has low female enrollment. The program has been trying to change this by promoting itself, for instance, to schools of nursing. All information sessions feature prominent alumnae, as does literature on the program. The school even keeps track of how many cases have "female decision-makers" —real-life ones, not plants. (It's 13%.) In fact, whenever the faculty polls the students, they find that the women rate their satisfaction with the program slightly higher than the men do. Says one female student: "I'm coming from an engineering background so the representation of women was in fact less in my undergrad and work than at Ivey, so it hasn't affected me either way. The classroom environment in my opinion is equally supportive of women as men."

Profs, Programs, and Particulars

Since its inception, the Ivey MBA has kept to its goal of producing general managers. But increasingly, general managers need to understand the global component of business. The

MBA program has responded by adding courses that provide a global perspective. "Not international business," says Gandz, "but understanding business as a global entity." Some recent additions to the curriculum are several mini-courses on doing business in Mexico, Eastern Europe, and Southeast Asia, and a required course on the Global Environment of Business.

A-list Alumni

- Mark Arthur MBA '80: President and Chief Investment Officer, Royal Bank Investment Management Inc.
- Umberto Angeloni MBA '79: CEO, Brioni, Penne, Italy
- Rob Ritchie MBA '70: President and CEO, CP Rail System
- Donald Triggs MBA '68: President, Vincor International
- William Stinson MBA '68: President and CEO, Canadian Pacific Ltd.

During the first year of the program, MBA students follow a program of study that's fairly similar to the first year of the HBA: three cases a day, five days a week, in the basic building blocks of a management degree. Case situations don't exist in a vacuum, so a case in finance class may draw upon what students have learned in accounting or operations. "We're not allowed to be myopic in any of our classes," says a student.

The second year of the program is devoted to electives and the business policy class, a semester-long project that has students working extensively with a company. In September 1997 the MBA added a stream in consulting; further streams are planned for the areas of financial services and entrepreneurship.

The MBA benefits from the close proximity of Western's executive wing. "There's a symbiotic relationship between the MBA and the executive development programs," says a prof.

Many profs will walk out of an executive class with senior level participants and into an MBA class.

> Profs are accessible and get high marks for teaching and caring about students, as well as bringing real-world experience into the classroom. "The single thing I've enjoyed most is the faculty," says a student.

Living It Up

Many students in the program are married and a lot of socializing goes on over dinner at people's houses. The MBA students used to be divided into four sections instead of three. Around that time, Section 5, composed of spouses of students in the program, sprang up. Still known by that name, the group acts as a support team for spouses and runs social activities. People also get together to play laser tag and go to the Grand Theatre in town. On-campus hangouts are the grad pub for lunch and The Wave, in the university community centre. Students congregate at The Spoke every Friday night. The Shotgun and Joe Kool's are two other favoured watering holes.

The club situation in the MBA is distinguished by actually having more people applying for spots than there are positions. "There are about 40 applications to be convenors for 25 to 30 positions," says a student. About a third of the student body is heavily involved in clubs. All clubs in the business school are run by the MBA Association. Other MBA association activities are a two-day forum to which business leaders are invited, a graduate business conference, various social events, and peer support for exchange students. Participation in case competitions is co-ordinated through the MBA association. The association also has a tie-in to various community services, such as a blood drive and a food drive. The MBA association puts out a résumé book with the help of career services.

The Payoff

Ivey's career services was restructured recently and now has a large staff of eight full-time people. Three people have expertise in financial services, consulting and technology, and consumer goods and other industries, respectively. More emphasis is being placed on targeting students early on to help them figure out their career path and make the right decisions. Students are pleased with the efforts of career services. "It's really obvious here that placement is a big priority and a lot of time and effort goes into building long-term relationships with employers," says a student.

The office managed to survey 92% of the class of '98 and found that 91% had found employment within three months of graduation. The highest proportion of grads (26%) ends up in consulting; investment banking accounts for 17%; manufacturing for 17%; and other financial services for 12%. Most grads (60%) head to Toronto; the rest of Canada accounts for another 17%; and 4% end up on Wall Street. The average starting salary is $74,000.

Executive MBA

Ivey offers two Executive MBA programs, one in Mississauga, Ontario, and the other in seven sites nationwide through videoconferencing. Sites are in the following cities: Markham, Ottawa, and London in Ontario; Vancouver and Burnaby in BC; Calgary; and Montreal. Admission requirements are the same for both programs. Applicants need a minimum of eight years of managerial experience; the average is 15 years. Mississauga classes are held every week on alternating Fridays and Saturdays. Videoconference classes are held every two weeks on back-to-back Fridays and Saturdays. No classes are held in July and August.

The Mississauga program has four one-week residential sessions at the beginning of each term; the videoconference program has a two-week residential session at the start of first term, and three one-week sessions at the beginning of the other three terms. In addition there is one long weekend per term which is held somewhere in Western Canada. The residential parts of both programs are held at Spencer Hall in London, the former home of Major General Spencer who donated his mansion to Western.

The EMBA curriculum is similar to that of the MBA program, minus many of the electives. Everyone takes 19 courses over two years. In addition to course work, everyone must complete a functional project, a general management project in their sponsoring organization, and a best practices management project, which often takes an international perspective.

This is the way the videoconferencing class works. Each site has about 10 students in a room that makes them look like contestants on Reach for the Top. There are two large TV screens, one showing the prof lecturing in London and the other showing any documents or calculations that the prof is using. When a student asks a question, the prof disappears, the screen zooms in on the student and the prof reappears in a small square in a corner of the screen.

> What's unique about taking an EMBA through videoconferencing is the particular classroom culture it fosters. "You have to learn to listen differently and you have to use your speaking time wisely. It's your 15 minutes of fame," says one student. Participants can discuss things in class without the prof hearing, since communication is two-way only if the student presses on the intercom button. There's also the cross-Canada perspective that you get from people at other sites.

How does Ivey's videoconferencing EMBA differ from Queen's? Per site, the groups are slightly larger at Western, and the case-study method imparts a very different feeling to the classroom. But the biggest difference is that the lecturer at Western sees all seven sites at once. Western's classroom feels more efficient while Queen's feels more informal.

The Bottom Line

Gradventures

Interactive Simulations Inc. (Michael Needham MBA '68)

What the Judges Think

1997 Concordia University MBA International Case Competition: 1st place

Foreign Affairs

Ivey has exchanges with more than 23 institutions in other countries and one with the École des Hautes Études Commerciales in Montreal. One faculty member in the school of business is responsible for scouring the world for appropriate academic exchange partners. Typically there is only one school per country and it's a school whose standards, in the faculty's view, most closely approximate Western's.

Aside from academic exchanges, students may spend three weeks in May teaching in the LEADER (students Leading Education And Development in Eastern euRope) project which sends MBAs to Eastern Europe to teach business skills to officials and aspiring entrepreneurs. Since 1994 a handful of students have also participated in the Business in Beijing Program, which has students teaching a three-week credit course at Tsinghua University.

Money for Nothing

A few MBA students work as teaching assistants and research assistants. The salary varies with the professor. Scholarships have been increasing steadily over the past couple of years.

Options

- Joint MBA/LLB
- PhD

Contacts

Richard Ivey School of Business • The University of Western Ontario • 1151 Richmond St. N. • London, ON • N6A 3K7 • (519) 661-3206 • www.ivey.uwo.ca

UNIVERSITY OF WESTERN ONTARIO—VITAL STATISTICS	
total university enrollment	25,026
total full-time undergrad enrollment	18,949
number of full-time professors in the school of business	78
number of part-time professors	8
number of women professors	20
MBA	
full-time enrollment	450
part-time enrollment	none
size of entering class	210
women students	25%
out-of-province students	42%
international students	21%
students straight from undergrad	none
average age	29
annual tuition	$8,000
annual tuition for international students	$14,000
length of program	2 years
number of applications	926

number of acceptances	300
cut-off grade for admission	70%
average grade of admittees	78%
average GMAT	632
years of work experience required	2
average years of work experience	5
size of core classes	70
size of electives	20 to 50
classes taught by full-time faculty	100%
grads employed within three months of graduation	91%
number of on-campus recruiters	273
grads hired through placement office	N/A
average starting salary	$74,000
what employment figures are based on	92% of the class of '98

Executive MBA in Mississauga

enrollment	106
women students	30%
average age	37
average GMAT	N/A
years of work experience required	8
average years of work experience	16
cost of program	$54,000

Videoconference Executive MBA

enrollment	57
women students	32%
average age	38
average GMAT	554
years of work experience required	8
average years of work experience	16
cost of program	$52,000

Wilfrid Laurier University

It's a pity that the School of Business and Economics at Wilfrid Laurier University has to be in the same province as Queen's and Western. Despite a good quality year-long MBA program (the oldest one-year program in Canada), the clientele of the university is still largely regional. Outside Ontario, WLU gets overlooked by prospective students; inside it doesn't yet get the recruiters of its more pedigreed rivals. Talk to students and you get the feeling that they expect great things in the school's future.

Since its founding in 1966, the SBE has aimed to offer balanced programs with a strong dose of applied business skills. Case study is the main method of instruction in the MBA. In fact Laurier produces more case studies than anyone in Canada except Western. Lately the SBE has been extending its reach: it now has two part-time MBA programs, one in Sarnia, which began in 1996, and one on Toronto's Lakeshore, which it has offered with Humber College since 1997. It is set to begin offering a joint MBA with the Society of Certified Management Accountants of Canada in 2000.

Laurier is in downtown Kitchener-Waterloo. Most of the campus is situated within the bounds of four streets. The building style is functional (read: squat and brown). The SBE has the Frank C. Peters Building to itself. There's no campus green to speak of and most of the wide-open spaces, with the exception of the football field, are student or staff parking lots. But students congregate on the grassy knolls between the buildings, and there's usually a crowd in the courtyard outside the Student Union Building when the weather warms up.

MBA

Getting In

In 1997-98 the MBA received 260 applications for full-time study, of which it accepted 105. For part-time study, there were 89 applications; 45 were admitted. The minimum grade for admission is a B; the average grade of admitted students is a B+. The program requires two years of work experience; most students have closer to eight. Laurier revised its one-year program in 1994. Before the revision, the program catered primarily to engineers and other technical professions. In the new program, technical has a broader meaning—nurses, architects, and engineers all qualify.

A-list Alumni

- Michael Daunt MBA '96: Five-time "Jeopardy" champion
- Don Steward MBA '93: Director of National Accounts, Laidlaw Inc.
- Patricia Krajewski MBA '90: Vice-President, Training and Development, The Bank of Nova Scotia
- John Lauer MBA '78: President, Agribusiness, J.M. Schneiders

Atmospherics

These days it's hard to find an MBA program that doesn't pay lip service to the soft skills. Even so, Laurier stands out: getting along with people is practically part of the curriculum. When he's asked who should stay away from this program, Gene Deszca, director of the MBA, responds immediately, "someone with sharp elbows." Adds a student: "I was intimidated about being in an MBA program, but the professors weren't promoting an adversarial relationship."

> Students spend a weekend kayaking and mountain climbing three weeks into the program. This event is meant to force them to work together as teams and give them a break from courses, but it's also designed to "dispel the macho image," says Deszca. "If you're 120 pounds and agile you're much better off than someone who's built like a football player."
>
> All that friendliness can make one feel a bit surly, especially when it shows up as massive amounts of group work. "You're in a 12-month program, you're working your butt off, and you sometimes feel you could have done it twice as fast alone," says an alum, adding, "If you don't like to work with people, then don't go to Laurier."

Students praise the MBA office for the personal attention it lavishes on students. "I felt like a person every time I talked to them," says one grad. Mug shots of students are up on the wall and profs use them to learn names. The faculty is "really receptive" to student concerns. "They've made changes from last year to this year," says an alum.

Profs, Programs, and Particulars

During first semester, all courses are taught in integrated modules. These receive high marks for co-ordination and organization. "They were integrated in more than just name," one student says. Almost all classes are taught in seminar format and group work is emphasized.

In second semester, the integration disappears. The semester is divided between business electives, of which there are about 40, and the applied business course, also known as the adopt-a-company project. (Managing your daytimer turns out to be one of the most stressful things about the semester, since in addition to your classes, you've got to schedule in group work.)

The adopt-a-company project varies widely from team to team. One student worked with a financial services organization that wanted to refine its corporate strategy. Another worked with an entrepreneur who wanted to get into auto-parts marketing. Students prepare the proprietary work for the company and present it at the end of the project.

Between second and third semester, some students go on the travel option. In 1995 a group of MBA students went to Chile, Argentina, and Brazil to conduct research for a book on the possibilities of doing business in those countries. "We had meetings with businesses that could mop up the floor with some of the companies we think kick butt up here. It's very easy to read about it in a newspaper or see it on TV, but it really hits home when you go into a factory and see the level of sophistication of their operations," says one participant.

> Students must also spend at least 40 hours working for a non-profit organization. Some have worked for such organizations as the Canadian Cancer Society, the Graduate Students Association at Laurier, St. John's Soup Kitchen, and Jessie's, a program for pregnant teenagers.

What's it like to cram everything into one year? "At the beginning of the year, one prof drew a time line on the board and explained that for every hour in class, you should spend three hours in study. When the diagram was finished, we ended up owing them time," says one student. "The learning curve is steep, and you assimilate a lot of stuff in a short time," adds another student. The material becomes applicable almost immediately.

Living It Up

There's not much time for social life around the school. As one married student says, "Make a choice. Do you want to get involved or do you want to have a family?" Some popular hangouts are: Wilf's, especially around the pool table; the MBA lounge and the MBA computer room in the Peter's Building; and The Fox and Pheasant, a pub just up the street from the SBE.

The Payoff

Laurier alumni are just starting to reach a critical mass, which should make them better known to recruiters. One alumnus described the placement service for MBA students as not equipped to deal with candidates who have already held three or four jobs, adding, "These people aren't looking for a job as assistant product manager. Career services should look more at other options, such as headhunters."

Laurier surveys MBAs one year after graduation. The career centre managed to contact 36 of the 78 members of the class of 1995 and 1996 and found that 90% were employed. The average starting salary was $58,800. Twenty-five percent were employed in general management; 15% in sales and marketing; 9% in operations; and 9% in information systems.

> **Sarnia MBA and Laurier on the Lakeshore**
>
> Laurier does not offer an Executive MBA. Instead it offers two part-time programs, one in Sarnia and one on Toronto's Lakeshore. They are identical versions of the one-year MBA designed to fit a weekend format. Students take classes two weekends a month for 10 months of the year and have July and August off. The program lasts four years. The format means that the course integration of the first semester of the MBA can be maintained and that students' lives are less chaotic than in an EMBA program.

The Bottom Line

Gradventures

Hollend Furnishings Ltd. (Rhonda Hollend MBA '89)

Money for Nothing

Between 50% and 60% of the MBA class has some form of funding. Each year, 12 to 20 people receive WLU graduate scholarships, ranging from $1,000 to $3,000. The higher an applicant's marks, the more money is awarded. In addition to the WLU scholarships, there are eight other scholarships, usually funded by industry donors, ranging from $500 to $2,000. Some scholarships are available for part-time study. The SBE appoints a few research assistants every year; these are awarded on the basis of need not performance.

Contacts

School of Business and Economics • Wilfrid Laurier University • 75 University Ave. W. • Waterloo, ON • N2L 3C5 • (519) 884-0710 • www.wlu.ca/~wwwsbe/

WILFRID LAURIER UNIVERSITY—VITAL STATISTICS

total university enrollment	7,766
total full-time undergrad enrollment	5,328
number of full-time business professors in the SBE	83
number of part-time professors	20
number of women professors	19

MBA

full-time enrollment	83
part-time enrollment	103
size of entering class	78 full-time; 50 part-time
women students	40% full-time; 48% part-time
out-of-province students	0.4%
international students	6%
students straight from undergrad	none
average age	32
total tuition	$5,346
total tuition for international students	$10,500
length of program	1 year
number of applications	260 full-time; 89 part-time
number of acceptances	105 full-time; 45 part-time
cut-off grade for admission	B
average grade of admitted students	B+
average GMAT	600
years of work experience required	2
average years of work experience	8

size of core classes	50
size of electives	40
classes taught by full-time faculty	90%
grads employed within a year of graduation	86%
number of on-campus recruiters	230 for all programs at Laurier
grads hired through placement	N/A
average starting salary	$48,130 (based on 23 responses)
what employment figures are based on	62 out of 70 grads of the class of '95

Sarnia MBA

enrollment	40
women students	36%
average age	36
average GMAT	575
years of work experience required	2
average years of work experience	12
cost of program	$26,000

Laurier on the Lakeshore

enrollment	46
women students	30%
average age	35
average GMAT	565
years of work experience required	2
average years of work experience	11
cost of program	$28,000

University of Windsor

If you are young, school-smart, and confident that an MBA is the logical step after an undergraduate degree, the University of Windsor wants you. Of course they'll take you if you're grizzled and have years of work experience, but you'll be an anomaly. With an average age of 25, Windsor MBAs are the babies of Canada's MBA scene. Nor are they likely to grow any older: like McMaster University, Windsor is moving to make its very successful co-op program an even bigger part of the MBA.

Like students at McMaster University in Hamilton, that other industrial city in Ontario, students at the University of Windsor are ambivalent about the city after which their university is named. "People have this mindset about Windsor, but it's not true. They say it's the end of the road, that we're one end of Canada, so it's not so much a Canadian university," says a student. "People in this province tend to judge everything by what's in the Golden Horseshoe," complains another. But there are benefits to being in Windsor. Students can take courses at nearby Wayne State University in Detroit and at other

Michigan universities. And with Ford Motor Co., General Motors Corp., and Chrysler Ltd. a stone's throw away, this is a reasonable place for someone who wants to get in with an auto company.

Business is a high-profile faculty. Drive off the 401, take the road to the bridge, and the 1992 Odette Business Building is one of the first things you see, like "a transformer about to take off," says an arts alumna. The building has top-notch classrooms and computer labs and is so spiffy it clashes somewhat with the rest of the 1857 campus. It's not unusual to have students cite Odette as one of the strengths of the program and not even blush while saying it.

MBA

Getting In

The MBA received 500 applications for entry in 1998 and accepted 150. The cut-off average for admission is 70%; the average grade is about 75%. Students aren't required to have any work experience and 90% of students come straight from an undergraduate program.

The MBA program has several streams. In addition to the regular stream, the co-op stream, and the part-time stream, there is a fast-track MBA for undergrads who have a four-year business degree. These students complete the second year of the regular MBA and graduate in one year.

A-list Alumni

- Patricia Hunt MBA '92: Windsor Harbormaster
- Dwight Duncan MBA '89: MPP, Windsor-Walkerville
- Carl Nanni MBA '76: Vice-President, Marketing, Kraft General Foods Canada Inc.
- Thomas Knowlton MBA '70: President, Kellogg North America
- Stephan T. Bellringer MBA '69: President and CEO, Orca Bay Sports and Entertainment

Atmospherics

With an entering class of 52, Windsor's MBA program is small and close-knit. "Students in the MBA have a lot of spirit. We're always able to get a good crowd out," says a second-year MBA/LLB student. Many students agree that the No. 1 thing about the program is the people. "Professors are pretty laid-back here. They're not at all pompous," says another student.

Profs, Programs, and Particulars

Windsor's revamped two-year MBA started in September 1996. First semester starts with a two-week introduction to business that deals primarily with the Canadian business scene and how it compares with other economies. The intro also has an interpersonal dynamics component where students do team-building and conflict-resolution exercises. Still in teams, the students spend the rest of the semester learning the functional areas of business. A business simulation runs concurrently and helps integrate the material. Second semester is also modular and integrated, but students may choose their own teams.

In second year, students may specialize in finance, accounting, marketing, management science, management and labour studies, or small business/entrepreneurship. Finance and marketing are strong, students say, but accounting is weak, possibly because of low student interest. There is the opportunity for students to write a major paper or a thesis, both of which require a defence.

Gradventures

- Compurent (Mark Meldrum MBA '94)
- Second Byte (Mark Meldrum)
- Video Cube (Wayne Parent MBA '85)

For students not in co-op, there are some opportunities for contact with the business community. "In co-op we do it best, but we're trying to do it in the other streams as well," says the former director of the MBA. There is the possibility of students taking unpaid internships in non-profit organizations. The Business Resource Centre, the small business consulting group at Windsor, allows students to work as consultants for cash and credit. The Office of Automotive Research and Training (OART) is a resource for the automotive industry that provides consulting, seminars, and training programs.

Co-op

In the new program, 90% of MBA students are in co-op. In addition to meeting the requirements for the general MBA, students go through an interview to get into the co-op program. "What we're looking for is exactly what the employer is looking for," says Dana Tonus, director of co-op services. The program admits about 40 of the 50 who apply. All co-op students must attend 27 mandatory workshops, a minimum of seven per term. (If you miss a workshop, you have to make up for it with a 1,000-word essay.)

Windsor recently reduced the number of co-op terms from three to two. Students now go on their first work term after first semester. The placement rate is 95%. Ninety percent of employers are in the Windsor/Ottawa corridor, with the majority in Toronto. The remaining 10% are in BC, Calgary, Edmonton, Halifax, and Detroit. The majority of jobs fall in the banking, manufacturing, and high-tech industries; the smallest number, in government. Average work-term salary is $525 a week for 16 weeks.

> **Most popular co-ops:** finance positions, particularly in investments. Chrysler, Ford, and GM all post, but the Ford jobs are the ones that people want.

Windsor recently added a novel feature to its co-op program. Every student now has a faculty mentor who visits the student on-site and attends any presentations the student might do. "We want our professors to be in contact with industry and we want students to develop a solid rapport with a faculty member," says Tonus.

Living It Up

Detroit is the playground of choice. Every Thursday night, MBAs head out to Cobo Joe's, and every Saturday night, to Wheelers. In addition to the bars (which all take Canadian money), there are several sports venues for baseball, basketball, and football, not to mention the State Theater and the Fox Theater. By contrast, Windsor is a little staid. "There isn't much to do in Windsor. I miss the traffic in Toronto—I know it sounds sick," complains an MBA student. Some popular pubs in Windsor are the Penalty Box, Woody's, Cadillac Jacks, and Howl at the Moon. Everyone goes to the Grad House, the campus pub.

The Payoff

Career services keeps close tabs on its co-op grads. It surveys all of them and can safely boast that 100% are employed within six months of graduation at an average salary of $45,000. About 30% of co-op grads start a permanent job with their co-op employer. As for the handful of non-co-op students, the office conducts a phone survey which has a 90% response rate. Of those contacted, 70% had found employment within six months of graduation at an average salary of $39,500. Excluding co-op employers, the office attracts about 20 on-campus recruiters. The three top employers are the manufacturing, banking, and finance industries, in that order.

The Bottom Line

What the Judges Think
1992 MBA International Case Competition at Concordia: 3rd place

Foreign Affairs
The faculty has exchanges with five universities in Sweden, the Netherlands, Germany, France, and Mexico. Students may also participate in the Ontario Regional Program that sends students to study in Germany, France, Italy, or Spain.

Money for Nothing
The school of business offers 10 MBA scholarships worth between $500 and $5,000. Forty students work as TAs or research assistants at a salary of $2,240 per semester.

Other Options
Joint MBA/LLB

Contacts
Faculty of Business Administration • University of Windsor • 401 Sunset Ave. • Windsor, ON • N9B 3P4 • (519) 973-7090 • www.uwindsor.ca/faculty/busad

UNIVERSITY OF WINDSOR—VITAL STATISTICS

total university enrollment	12,657
total full-time undergrad enrollment	8,943
number of full-time professors in the faculty of business	39
number of part-time professors	12
number of women professors	7

MBA

full-time enrollment	118
part-time enrollment	61
size of entering class	52
women students	39%
out-of-province students	5%
international students	10%
students straight from undergrad	90%
average age	25
annual tuition	$4,500
annual tuition for international students	$8,453
length of program	2 years; 1 year for business grads
number of applications	500
number of acceptances	150
cut-off grade for admission	70%
average grade of admitted students	75%
average GMAT	570
years of work experience required	none
average years of work experience	N/A

size of core classes	40 to 50
size of electives	10 to 40
classes taught by full-time faculty	99%
grads employed within six months of graduation	100% co-op; 70% non-co-op
number of on-campus recruiters	20
grads hired through placement	N/A
average starting salary	$42,500 co-op; $39,500 non-co-op
what employment figures are based on	100% of co-ops; 90% of non-co-ops

York University

At York's business school, you can study everything—commonplace subjects such as marketing or finance, but also any number of specializations such as arts and media administration or business and the environment. Many students come to the Schulich School of Business, the largest graduate school of management in Canada, because what they're interested in just isn't offered elsewhere.

They're also choosing this campus for its reputation as one of the top business schools in Canada and its close connections with the business community. The school, like many, has an advisory council, but every program in the school has its own advisory council as well. York now derives more revenue from executive training than any other Canadian business school. And if you're used to thinking of York as a fixture in the wilds of the Toronto suburb of Downsview, take another look. A few years ago, York opened its Downtown Management Centre in the former Toronto Stock Exchange, where many executive courses and some MBA courses are now held.

> In little over a decade, York has also become a leader in the field of international business. The first international MBA (IMBA) in Canada, founded in part on the principle that students should be able to speak the language and understand the culture of the foreign country in which they're doing business, started here in 1990. The school has a large selection of international exchanges, and its executive wing regularly brings in such esoteric groups as Russian metallurgists. Half the students in the full-time MBA program hail from abroad.

What's unusual about this success is that unlike other top business schools such as Western or the University of Toronto, York's has been around a mere 30 odd years. (The university itself was established in 1959.) While its contemporaries bemoan their youth, a recent York slogan claims, "No ivy on our walls. No cobwebs in our mind." Lack of ivy didn't stop the school from snaring a $15-million donation from mining magnate Seymour Schulich in 1995, at the time the largest donation ever to a Canadian university.

Urban myth #1: York's campus is so spread out because the buildings were meant to represent a dove with wings outstretched. Urban myth #2: York is so spread out because it was actually designed to be in Southern California. The truth is that construction started at two separate ends and money ran out in the 1970s before some of the middle buildings could be built. The campus does have a weirdly Southern Californian feel— lots of low, rectangular concrete buildings—except in winter when the wind whistles hideously between the buildings. Schulich is in a nondescript modern building, and there are ongoing plans to move the school to a bigger and better facility.

MBA

Getting In

In 1997-98 the MBA received 1,695 applications and accepted 839 of them. Applicants need an undergraduate degree with an average of B or more in the last two years of study. Work experience is preferred but not required, and the admissions office also considers extracurriculars, leadership qualities, and communication skills. Applicants to the IMBA must come in with language skills at the intermediate-high level in the language of the region they wish to study. The MBA accepts a small number of mature students without an undergraduate degree.

Atmospherics

Because the MBA program is so large, there tends not to be the close atmosphere that one finds in smaller programs. "Most of the time you have to make an effort to mingle, there are so many people. The onus is on you to take the initiative," says a student. You can feel a bit like a cog, but since everything takes place in one building, "you do get a sense of belonging to a community," adds another. And in a place this big, there is the occasional bureaucratic horror.

The MBA has a large part-time population, and the school does a good job of catering to these students. It's easy to move between the part-time and full-time options, and it's fairly easy for part-timers to go on exchange. The program also offers the flexibility of different entry points: students may start in September and January. Because York runs on the trimester system, it hasn't had to consider offering a shorter MBA. It's always been possible for students to complete the regular MBA in 16 straight months.

Part-timers also bring in a lot of experience. "There are a lot of people that come straight through from undergrad. You don't get the perspective that you get from the part-time students," says a full-time MBA student.

Profs, Programs, and Particulars

York's regular two-year MBA was restructured in 1994. It's still a strong generalist program but there are numerous opportunities to specialize in second year. One of York's strengths is the sheer variety of courses—there are more than 90 electives to choose from. Students can concentrate on a functional area such as accounting, economics, finance, management science, marketing, organizational behaviour/industrial relations, or management/policy. Marketing and finance are very strong. Students praise the policy area as well: "We have some of the top policy profs at York, but it's underpublicized."

More recent and unusual concentrations allow students to focus either on a particular sector or management issue. These include arts and media administration, financial services, public management, real property development, business and the environment, entrepreneurial studies, international business, voluntary sector management, and most recently, financial engineering. Students in arts and media administration and real property development can graduate with a diploma in those areas. Arts and media students must participate in an internship. There is also a new joint MBA and Master of Fine Arts, a natural complement to the arts and media administration diploma.

A-list Alumni

- Rick Broadhead MBA '96: Co-author with Jim Carroll of the best-selling *Canadian Internet Handbook*
- Terence G. Kawaja MBA LLB '89: Vice-President, Mergers and Acquisitions, Salomon Brothers Inc., New York City
- Julie White MBA '84: President, Trillium Foundation
- Paul Howes MBA '84: President, Merck Frosst Canada Inc.
- Sheelagh Whittaker MBA '75: President, EDS Canada

The IMBA is an intensive program, 24 months non-stop, where students acquire expertise in a particular region of the world. Students may choose among Eastern Europe, Latin America, Asia Pacific, North America (for visa students only), Southern Asia, Southeast Asia, and Western Europe, or do an independent study on another region. All students come in able to speak the language and by the time they graduate they must speak it at the advanced-high level. "We're breaking down the psychological barrier to behaving in a global environment," says Dean Dezsö Horvath. Aside from core and elective courses, students must attend international business seminars.

A major component of the IMBA is the required three-month internship abroad. The placement office will provide some help in securing internships and there is also the alumni network to tap into, but generally students must find their jobs on their own. "A lot of people end up having office jobs," says one student.

The IMBA and MBA share Skills Week, many of the core courses, and the strategy field study. The further the IMBA students get into their program, the fewer courses they share with the regular MBA. Skills Week is orientation, professional development, and intro to computing and library services all rolled into one. Material has been added on the management of diversity

The strategy study is a six-month team consulting project undertaken in the second semester of second year. Each team has a trio of professors who act as mentors. An increasing number of strategy studies have taken place abroad. A recent program has teams from Schulich, Wharton at the University of Pennsylvania, and the Rekanati School in Israel working on marketing plans for six Israeli firms.

> **Gradventures**
>
> - Arbor International (Leon Cherniak MBA '83)
> - Investor Economics Ltd. (Earl Bederman MBA '73)
> - Sunrise Records (Malcolm Perlman MBA '69)
> - Trimark Investment Management (Robert C. Krembil MBA '71)

Quality of teaching is high with the odd exception. Students single out the part-time lecturers for praise. "They brought more knowledge, life, and fun to the class. They'd say, 'Here's stuff that's happening to my client,'" says an alum. "I had excellent profs who had day jobs like me," adds a former part-timer.

Living It Up

The Financial Poste is, grudgingly, the hangout of default—"I don't really want to listen to CHMY and eat junk food," says one reluctant customer. The Osgoode Hall cafeteria is right next door, and some MBAs take refuge there. There is a grad lounge as well in Schulich. Off-campus hangouts are Kelsey's, the Cock 'n Bull, and the Bohemian. IMBA students organize nights out to restaurants of the regions that they're studying.

There are a large number of clubs for students to choose from. The major ones are the Graduate Business Council (GBC), the Marketing Club, the Finance Association, the Real Property Development Association, the Arts and Media Management Club, Business and the Environment, the Entrepreneurs Club, the Joint MBA/LLB Society, and the Sports and Business Club, which is one of the most popular new clubs. *The FASTrack* is the MBA newspaper. Every year, MBA students put on the Canadian Graduate Business Conference. The yearly CEO Back to Campus event, organized by the school, brings in 100 select CEOs to hobnob with MBAs.

The Payoff

Business Career Services (BCS) is particularly good at helping students interested in finance and marketing positions, students say. There is always a good selection of banks, accounting firms, and packaged goods firms. It isn't quite as bountiful in areas like arts and media administration, but the few students in this area often get jobs through internship employers. "We have so many programs, that there are some that don't get their share," says one student. There aren't too many international postings either, though IMBA students do find jobs at the same rate as regular MBAs.

All MBA students may participate in the alumni mentorship program which matches up students and alumni. The office provides the same services for MBAs as for undergrads. According to BCS, 45% of students find employment through the office. The office surveyed 181 students out of the 474 graduates of the class of '98 and found that within six months of graduation, 96% of them had found permanent employment, at an average starting salary of $76,000. Thirty-two percent of grads took positions in finance, 22% in marketing, 15% in consulting, and 12% in sales. If postings and just-in-time hirings are added to the number of on-campus recruiters, the total number of companies looking for business grads rises from 165 to 2,000.

The Bottom Line

Foreign Affairs

Schulich has more international exchanges than any other program at York. MBAs have access to exchanges with 24 universities in England, France, Germany, Italy, Norway, the Netherlands, Spain, Hong Kong, Korea, Japan, Thailand, Mexico, Argentina, Brazil, Venezuela, Chile, and Université Laval in Quebec.

Money for Nothing

MBA and IMBA students are eligible for 200 scholarships worth a total of $300,000. Awards range from $500 to $10,000.

Other Options

- Joint MBA/LLB
- Master of public administration
- Joint MBA/MFA

Contacts

Schulich School of Business • York University • North York, ON• M3J 1P3 • (416) 736-5855 • www.bus.yorku.ca

YORK UNIVERSITY—VITAL STATISTICS	
total university enrollment	38,217
total full-time undergrad enrollment	26,000
number of full-time professors in Schulich	77
number of part-time professors	76
number of women professors	44
MBA	
full-time enrollment	450 MBA; 100 IMBA
part-time enrollment	700 MBA; none in IMBA
size of entering class	270 in the full-time MBA 260 in the part-time MBA 50 in the IMBA

women students	38%
out-of-province students	20%
international students	50%
students straight from undergrad	20%
average age	29
tuition per term	$1,815 full-time; $908 part-time
tuition for international students	$8,062 full-time; $4,030 part-time
length of program	16 months MBA; 24 months IMBA
number of applications	1,695
number of acceptances	839
cut-off grade for admission	B
average grade of admittees	B+
average GMAT	610 to 620
years of work experience required	none
average years of work experience	5
size of core classes	50
size of electives	25
classes taught by full-time faculty	65%
grads employed within six months of graduation	96%
number of on-campus recruiters	165
grads hired through placement office	45%
average starting salary	$76,000
what employment figures are based on	181 out of 472 grads of the class of '98